ON THE HOLY SPIRIT

DE SPIRITU SANCTO

By SAINT BASIL

Translated by BLOMFIELD JACKSON

On the Holy Spirit
By Saint Basil
Translated by Blomfield Jackson

Print ISBN 13: 978-1-4209-7060-9
eBook ISBN 13: 978-1-4209-7061-6

This edition copyright © 2020. Digireads.com Publishing.

All rights reserved. No part of this publication may be reproduced, distributed, or transmitted in any form or by any means, including photocopying, recording, or other electronic or mechanical methods, without the prior written permission of the publisher, except in the case of brief quotations embodied in critical reviews and certain other noncommercial uses permitted by copyright law.

Cover Image: a detail of "St. Basil Dictating his Doctrine", by Francisco Herrera (1576-1656), c. 17th century, (oil on canvas) / Bridgeman Images.

Please visit *www.digireads.com*

CONTENTS

CHAPTER 1. PREFATORY REMARKS ON THE NEED OF EXACT INVESTIGATION OF THE MOST MINUTE PORTIONS OF THEOLOGY. 7

CHAPTER 2. THE ORIGIN OF THE HERETICS' CLOSE OBSERVATION OF SYLLABLES. 9

CHAPTER 3. THE SYSTEMATIC DISCUSSION OF SYLLABLES IS DERIVED FROM HEATHEN PHILOSOPHY. 10

CHAPTER 4. THAT THERE IS NO DISTINCTION IN THE SCRIPTURAL USE OF THESE SYLLABLES. 11

CHAPTER 5. THAT "THROUGH WHOM" IS SAID ALSO IN THE CASE OF THE FATHER, AND "OF WHOM" IN THE CASE OF THE SON AND OF THE SPIRIT. 12

CHAPTER 6. ISSUE JOINED WITH THOSE WHO ASSERT THAT THE SON IS NOT WITH THE FATHER, BUT AFTER THE FATHER. ALSO CONCERNING THE EQUAL GLORY. 15

CHAPTER 7. AGAINST THOSE WHO ASSERT THAT IT IS NOT PROPER FOR "WITH WHOM" TO BE SAID OF THE SON, AND THAT THE PROPER PHRASE IS "THROUGH WHOM." 19

CHAPTER 8. IN HOW MANY WAYS "THROUGH WHOM" IS USED; AND IN WHAT SENSE "WITH WHOM" IS MORE SUITABLE. EXPLANATION OF HOW THE SON RECEIVES A COMMANDMENT, AND HOW HE IS SENT. 20

CHAPTER 9. DEFINITIVE CONCEPTIONS ABOUT THE SPIRIT WHICH CONFORM TO THE TEACHING OF THE SCRIPTURES. 25

CHAPTER 10. AGAINST THOSE WHO SAY THAT IT IS NOT RIGHT TO RANK THE HOLY SPIRIT WITH THE FATHER AND THE SON. 26

CHAPTER 11. THAT THEY WHO DENY THE SPIRIT ARE TRANSGRESSORS. 28

CHAPTER 12. AGAINST THOSE WHO ASSERT THAT THE BAPTISM IN THE NAME OF THE FATHER ALONE IS SUFFICIENT. 29

CHAPTER 13. STATEMENT OF THE REASON WHY IN THE WRITINGS OF PAUL THE ANGELS ARE ASSOCIATED WITH THE FATHER AND THE SON. 30

CHAPTER 14. OBJECTION THAT SOME WERE BAPTIZED UNTO MOSES AND BELIEVED IN HIM, AND AN ANSWER TO IT; WITH REMARKS UPON TYPES............... 31

CHAPTER 15. REPLY TO THE SUGGESTED OBJECTION THAT WE ARE BAPTIZED "INTO WATER." ALSO CONCERNING BAPTISM............... 34

CHAPTER 16. THAT THE HOLY SPIRIT IS IN EVERY CONCEPTION SEPARABLE FROM THE FATHER AND THE SON, ALIKE IN THE CREATION OF PERCEPTIBLE OBJECTS, IN THE DISPENSATION OF HUMAN AFFAIRS, AND IN THE JUDGMENT TO COME. 36

CHAPTER 17. AGAINST THOSE WHO SAY THAT THE HOLY GHOST IS NOT TO BE NUMBERED WITH, BUT NUMBERED UNDER, THE FATHER AND THE SON. WHEREIN MOREOVER THERE IS A SUMMARY NOTICE OF THE FAITH CONCERNING RIGHT SUB-NUMERATION. 41

CHAPTER 18. IN WHAT MANNER IN THE CONFESSION OF THE THREE HYPOSTASES WE PRESERVE THE PIOUS DOGMA OF THE MONARCHIA. WHEREIN ALSO IS THE REFUTATION OF THEM THAT ALLEGE THAT THE SPIRIT IS SUBNUMERATED. 44

CHAPTER 19. AGAINST THOSE WHO ASSERT THAT THE SPIRIT OUGHT NOT TO BE GLORIFIED............... 47

CHAPTER 20. AGAINST THOSE WHO MAINTAIN THAT THE SPIRIT IS IN THE RANK NEITHER OF A SERVANT NOR OF A MASTER, BUT IN THAT OF THE FREE. 49

CHAPTER 21. PROOF FROM SCRIPTURE THAT THE SPIRIT IS CALLED LORD. 50

CHAPTER 22. ESTABLISHMENT OF THE NATURAL COMMUNION OF THE SPIRIT FROM HIS BEING, EQUALLY WITH THE FATHER AND THE SON, UNAPPROACHABLE IN THOUGHT. 52

CHAPTER 23. THE GLORIFYING OF THE ENUMERATION OF HIS ATTRIBUTES. 53

CHAPTER 24. PROOF OF THE ABSURDITY OF THE REFUSAL TO GLORIFY THE SPIRIT, FROM THE COMPARISON OF THINGS GLORIFIED IN CREATION. 54

CHAPTER 25. THAT SCRIPTURE USES THE WORDS "IN" OR "BY," ἐN, IN PLACE OF "WITH." WHEREIN ALSO IT IS PROVED THAT THE WORD "AND" HAS THE SAME FORCE AS "WITH." 56

CHAPTER 26. THAT THE WORD "IN," IN AS MANY SENSES AS IT BEARS, IS UNDERSTOOD OF THE SPIRIT. 58
CHAPTER 27. OF THE ORIGIN OF THE WORD "WITH," AND WHAT FORCE IT HAS. ALSO CONCERNING THE UNWRITTEN LAWS OF THE CHURCH. 61
CHAPTER 28. THAT OUR OPPONENTS REFUSE TO CONCEDE IN THE CASE OF THE SPIRIT THE TERMS WHICH SCRIPTURE USES IN THE CASE OF MEN, AS REIGNING TOGETHER WITH CHRIST. 65
CHAPTER 29. ENUMERATION OF THE ILLUSTRIOUS MEN IN THE CHURCH WHO IN THEIR WRITINGS HAVE USED THE WORD "WITH." 67
CHAPTER 30. EXPOSITION OF THE PRESENT STATE OF THE CHURCHES. 71

Chapter 1

Prefatory remarks on the need of exact investigation of the most minute portions of theology.

1. Your desire for information, my right well-beloved and most deeply respected brother Amphilochius, I highly commend, and not less your industrious energy. I have been exceedingly delighted at the care and watchfulness shown in the expression of your opinion that of all the terms concerning God in every mode of speech, not one ought to be left without exact investigation. You have turned to good account your reading of the exhortation of the Lord, "Every one that asks receives, and he that seeks finds," Luke 11:10, and by your diligence in asking might, I ween, stir even the most reluctant to give you a share of what they possess. And this in you yet further moves my admiration, that you do not, according to the manners of the most part of the men of our time, propose your questions by way of mere test, but with the honest desire to arrive at the actual truth. There is no lack in these days of captious listeners and questioners; but to find a character desirous of information, and seeking the truth as a remedy for ignorance, is very difficult. Just as in the hunter's snare, or in the soldier's ambush, the trick is generally ingeniously concealed, so it is with the inquiries of the majority of the questioners who advance arguments, not so much with the view of getting any good out of them, as in order that, in the event of their failing to elicit answers which chime in with their own desires, they may seem to have fair ground for controversy.

2. If "To the fool on his asking for wisdom, wisdom shall be reckoned," at how high a price shall we value "the wise hearer" who is quoted by the Prophet in the same verse with "the admirable counsellor"? It is right, I ween, to hold him worthy of all approbation, and to urge him on to further progress, sharing his enthusiasm, and in all things toiling at his side as he presses onwards to perfection. To count the terms used in theology as of primary importance, and to endeavour to trace out the hidden meaning in every phrase and in every syllable, is a characteristic wanting in those who are idle in the pursuit of true religion, but distinguishing all who get knowledge of "the mark" "of our calling;" Philippians 3:14, for what is set before us is, so far as is possible with human nature, to be made like God. Now without knowledge there can be no making like; and knowledge is not got without lessons. The beginning of teaching is speech, and syllables and words are parts of speech. It follows then that to investigate syllables is not to shoot wide of the mark, nor, because the questions raised are what might seem to some insignificant, are they on that account to be held unworthy of heed. Truth is always a quarry hard to hunt, and

therefore we must look everywhere for its tracks. The acquisition of true religion is just like that of crafts; both grow bit by bit; apprentices must despise nothing. If a man despise the first elements as small and insignificant, he will never reach the perfection of wisdom.

Yea and Nay are but two syllables, yet there is often involved in these little words at once the best of all good things, Truth, and that beyond which wickedness cannot go, a Lie. But why mention Yea and Nay? Before now, a martyr bearing witness for Christ has been judged to have paid in full the claim of true religion by merely nodding his head. If, then, this be so, what term in theology is so small but that the effect of its weight in the scales according as it be rightly or wrongly used is not great? Of the law we are told "not one jot nor one tittle shall pass away;" Matthew 5:18, how then could it be safe for us to leave even the least unnoticed? The very points which you yourself have sought to have thoroughly sifted by us are at the same time both small and great. Their use is the matter of a moment, and perhaps they are therefore made of small account; but, when we reckon the force of their meaning, they are great. They may be likened to the mustard plant which, though it be the least of shrub-seeds, yet when properly cultivated and the forces latent in its germs unfolded, rises to its own sufficient height.

If any one laughs when he sees our subtlety, to use the Psalmist's words, about syllables, let him know that he reaps laughter's fruitless fruit; and let us, neither giving in to men's reproaches, nor yet vanquished by their disparagement, continue our investigation. So far, indeed, am I from feeling ashamed of these things because they are small, that, even if I could attain to ever so minute a fraction of their dignity, I should both congratulate myself on having won high honor, and should tell my brother and fellow-investigator that no small gain had accrued to him therefrom.

While, then, I am aware that the controversy contained in little words is a very great one, in hope of the prize I do not shrink from toil, with the conviction that the discussion will both prove profitable to myself, and that my hearers will be rewarded with no small benefit. Wherefore now with the help, if I may so say, of the Holy Spirit Himself, I will approach the exposition of the subject, and, if you will, that I may be put in the way of the discussion, I will for a moment revert to the origin of the question before us.

3. Lately when praying with the people, and using the full doxology to God the Father in both forms, at one time "with the Son together with the Holy Ghost," and at another "through the Son in the Holy Ghost," I was attacked by some of those present on the ground that I was introducing novel and at the same time mutually contradictory terms.

You, however, chiefly with the view of benefiting them, or, if they are wholly incurable, for the security of such as may fall in with them, have expressed the opinion that some clear instruction ought to be published concerning the force underlying the syllables employed. I will therefore write as concisely as possible, in the endeavour to lay down some admitted principle for the discussion.

Chapter 2

The origin of the heretics' close observation of syllables.

4. The petty exactitude of these men about syllables and words is not, as might be supposed, simple and straightforward; nor is the mischief to which it tends a small one. There is involved a deep and covert design against true religion. Their pertinacious contention is to show that the mention of Father, Son, and Holy Ghost is unlike, as though they will thence find it easy to demonstrate that there is a variation in nature. They have an old sophism, invented by Aetius, the champion of this heresy, in one of whose Letters there is a passage to the effect that things naturally unlike are expressed in unlike terms, and, conversely, that things expressed in unlike terms are naturally unlike. In proof of this statement he drags in the words of the Apostle, "One God and Father of whom are all things,... and one Lord Jesus Christ by whom are all things." 1 Corinthians 8:6. "Whatever, then," he goes on, "is the relation of these terms to one another, such will be the relation of the natures indicated by them; and as the term 'of whom' is unlike the term 'by whom,' so is the Father unlike the Son." On this heresy depends the idle subtlety of these men about the phrases in question. They accordingly assign to God the Father, as though it were His distinctive portion and lot, the phrase "of Whom;" to God the Son they confine the phrase "by Whom;" to the Holy Spirit that of "in Whom," and say that this use of the syllables is never interchanged, in order that, as I have already said, the variation of language may indicate the variation of nature. Verily it is sufficiently obvious that in their quibbling about the words they are endeavouring to maintain the force of their impious argument.

By the term "of whom" they wish to indicate the Creator; by the term "through whom," the subordinate agent or instrument; by the term "in whom," or "in which," they mean to show the time or place. The object of all this is that the Creator of the universe may be regarded as of no higher dignity than an instrument, and that the Holy Spirit may appear to be adding to existing things nothing more than the contribution derived from place or time.

Chapter 3

The systematic discussion of syllables is derived from heathen philosophy.

5. They have, however, been led into this error by their close study of heathen writers, who have respectively applied the terms "of whom" and "through whom" to things which are by nature distinct. These writers suppose that by the term "of whom" or "of which" the matter is indicated, while the term "through whom" or "through which" represents the instrument, or, generally speaking, subordinate agency. Or rather—for there seems no reason why we should not take up their whole argument, and briefly expose at once its incompatibility with the truth and its inconsistency with their own teaching—the students of vain philosophy, while expounding the manifold nature of cause and distinguishing its peculiar significations, define some causes as principal, some as cooperative or con-causal, while others are of the character of "sine qua non," or indispensable.

For every one of these they have a distinct and peculiar use of terms, so that the maker is indicated in a different way from the instrument. For the maker they think the proper expression is "by whom," maintaining that the bench is produced "by" the carpenter; and for the instrument "through which," in that it is produced "through" or by means of adze and gimlet and the rest. Similarly they appropriate "of which" to the material, in that the thing made is "of" wood, while "according to which" shows the design, or pattern put before the craftsman. For he either first makes a mental sketch, and so brings his fancy to bear upon what he is about, or else he looks at a pattern previously put before him, and arranges his work accordingly. The phrase "on account of which" they wish to be confined to the end or purpose, the bench, as they say, being produced for, or on account of, the use of man. "In which" is supposed to indicate time and place. When was it produced? In this time. And where? In this place. And though place and time contribute nothing to what is being produced, yet without these the production of anything is impossible, for efficient agents must have both place and time. It is these careful distinctions, derived from unpractical philosophy and vain delusion, which our opponents have first studied and admired, and then transferred to the simple and unsophisticated doctrine of the Spirit, to the belittling of God the Word, and the setting at naught of the Divine Spirit. Even the phrase set apart by non-Christian writers for the case of lifeless instruments or of manual service of the meanest kind, I mean the expression "through or by means of which," they do not shrink from transferring to the Lord of all, and Christians feel no shame in applying

Saint Basil 11

to the Creator of the universe language belonging to a hammer or a saw.

Chapter 4

That there is no distinction in the scriptural use of these syllables.

6. We acknowledge that the word of truth has in many places made use of these expressions; yet we absolutely deny that the freedom of the Spirit is in bondage to the pettiness of Paganism. On the contrary, we maintain that Scripture varies its expressions as occasion requires, according to the circumstances of the case. For instance, the phrase "of which" does not always and absolutely, as they suppose, indicate the material, but it is more in accordance with the usage of Scripture to apply this term in the case of the Supreme Cause, as in the words "One God, of whom are all things," 1 Corinthians 8:6, and again, "All things of God." 1 Corinthians 11:12. The word of truth has, however, frequently used this term in the case of the material, as when it says "You shall make an ark of incorruptible wood;" and "You shall make the candlestick of pure gold;" Exodus 25:31, and "The first man is of the earth, earthy;" 1 Corinthians 15:47, and "You are formed out of clay as I am." But these men, to the end, as we have already remarked, that they may establish the difference of nature, have laid down the law that this phrase befits the Father alone. This distinction they have originally derived from heathen authorities, but here they have shown no faithful accuracy of limitation. To the Son they have in conformity with the teaching of their masters given the title of instrument, and to the Spirit that of place, for they say in the Spirit, and through the Son. But when they apply "of whom" to God they no longer follow heathen example, but go over, as they say, to apostolic usage, as it is said, "But of him are you in Christ Jesus," 1 Corinthians 1:30, and "All things of God." 1 Corinthians 11:12. What, then, is the result of this systematic discussion? There is one nature of Cause; another of Instrument; another of Place. So the Son is by nature distinct from the Father, as the tool from the craftsman; and the Spirit is distinct in so far as place or time is distinguished from the nature of tools or from that of them that handle them.

Chapter 5

That "through whom" is said also in the case of the Father, and "of whom" in the case of the Son and of the Spirit.

7. After thus describing the outcome of our adversaries' arguments, we shall now proceed to show, as we have proposed, that the Father does not first take "of whom" and then abandon "through whom" to the Son; and that there is no truth in these men's ruling that the Son refuses to admit the Holy Spirit to a share in "of whom" or in "through whom," according to the limitation of their new-fangled allotment of phrases. "There is one God and Father of whom are all things, and one Lord Jesus Christ through whom are all things." 1 Corinthians 8:6.

Yes; but these are the words of a writer not laying down a rule, but carefully distinguishing the hypostases.

The object of the apostle in thus writing was not to introduce the diversity of nature, but to exhibit the notion of Father and of Son as unconfounded. That the phrases are not opposed to one another and do not, like squadrons in war marshalled one against another, bring the natures to which they are applied into mutual conflict, is perfectly plain from the passage in question. The blessed Paul brings both phrases to bear upon one and the same subject, in the words "of him and through him and to him are all things." Romans 11:36. That this plainly refers to the Lord will be admitted even by a reader paying but small attention to the meaning of the words. The apostle has just quoted from the prophecy of Isaiah, "Who has known the mind of the Lord, or who has been his counsellor," and then goes on, "For of him and from him and to him are all things." That the prophet is speaking about God the Word, the Maker of all creation, may be learned from what immediately precedes: "Who has measured the waters in the hollow of his hand, and meted out heaven with the span, and comprehended the dust of the earth in a measure, and weighed the mountains in scales, and the hills in a balance? Who has directed the Spirit of the Lord, or being his counsellor has taught him?" Isaiah 40:12-13. Now the word "who" in this passage does not mean absolute impossibility, but rarity, as in the passage "Who will rise up for me against the evil doers?" and "What man is he that desires life?" and "Who shall ascend into the hill of the Lord?" So is it in the passage in question, "Who has directed [lxx., known] the Spirit of the Lord, or being his counsellor has known him?" "For the Father loves the Son and shows him all things." John 5:20. This is He who holds the earth, and has grasped it with His hand, who brought all things to order and adornment, who poised the hills in their places, and measured the waters, and gave to all things in the universe their proper rank, who encompasses the whole of heaven with but a small portion of His power, which, in a figure, the prophet calls a span. Well then did the apostle add "Of him and through him and to him are all things." Romans 11:38. For of Him, to all things that are, comes the cause of their being, according to the will of God the Father. Through Him all things have their continuance and constitution, for He created all things, and metes out to each severally what is necessary for its health and preservation. Wherefore to Him all things are turned, looking with irresistible longing and unspeakable affection to "the author," Acts 3:15, and maintainer "of" their "life," as it is written "The eyes of all wait upon you," and again, "These wait all upon you," and "You open your hand, and satisfy the desire of every living thing."

8. But if our adversaries oppose this our interpretation, what argument will save them from being caught in their own trap?

For if they will not grant that the three expressions "of him" and "through him" and "to him" are spoken of the Lord, they cannot but be applied to God the Father. Then without question their rule will fall through, for we find not only "of whom," but also "through whom" applied to the Father. And if this latter phrase indicates nothing derogatory, why in the world should it be confined, as though conveying the sense of inferiority, to the Son? If it always and everywhere implies ministry, let them tell us to what superior the God of glory and Father of the Christ is subordinate.

They are thus overthrown by their own selves, while our position will be on both sides made sure. Suppose it proved that the passage refers to the Son, "of whom" will be found applicable to the Son. Suppose on the other hand it be insisted that the prophet's words relate to God, then it will be granted that "through whom" is properly used of God, and both phrases have equal value, in that both are used with equal force of God. Under either alternative both terms, being employed of one and the same Person, will be shown to be equivalent. But let us revert to our subject.

9. In his Epistle to the Ephesians the apostle says, "But speaking the truth in love, may grow up into him in all things, which is the head, even Christ; from whom the whole body fitly joined together and compacted by that which every joint supplies, according to the effectual working in the measure of every part, makes increase of the body." Ephesians 4:15-16.

And again in the Epistle to the Colossians, to them that have not the knowledge of the Only Begotten, there is mention of him that holds "the head," that is, Christ, "from which all the body by joints and bands having nourishment ministered increases with the increase of God." Colossians 2:19. And that Christ is the head of the Church we have learned in another passage, when the apostle says "gave him to be the head over all things to the Church," Ephesians 1:22. and "of his fullness have all we received." John 1:16. And the Lord Himself says "He shall take of mine, and shall show it unto you." 1 John 16:15. In a word, the diligent reader will perceive that "of whom" is used in diverse manners. For instance, the Lord says, "I perceive that virtue is gone out of me." Similarly we have frequently observed "of whom" used of the Spirit. "He that sows to the spirit," it is said, "shall of the spirit reap life everlasting." Galatians 6:8. John too writes, "Hereby we know that he abides in us by (ἐκ) the spirit which he has given us." 1 John 3:24. "That which is conceived in her," says the angel, "is of the Holy Ghost," Matthew 1:20, and the Lord says "that which is born of the spirit is spirit." John 3:6. Such then is the case so far.

10. It must now be pointed out that the phrase "through whom" is admitted by Scripture in the case of the Father and of the Son and of the Holy Ghost alike. It would indeed be tedious to bring forward evidence of this in the case of the Son, not only because it is perfectly well known, but because this very point is made by our opponents. We now show that "through whom" is used also in the case of the Father. "God is faithful," it is said, "by whom (δι' οὗ) you were called unto the fellowship of his Son," 1 Corinthians 1:9, and "Paul an apostle of Jesus Christ by (διά) the will of God;" and again, "Wherefore you are no more a servant, but a son; and if a son, then an heir through God." And "like as Christ was raised up from the dead by (διά) the glory of God the Father." Isaiah, moreover, says, "Woe unto them that make deep counsel and not through the Lord;" and many proofs of the use of this phrase in the case of the Spirit might be adduced. "God has revealed him to us," it is said, "by (διά) the spirit;" 1 Corinthians 2:10, and in another place, "That good thing which was committed unto you keep by (διά) the Holy Ghost;" 2 Timothy 1:14, and again, "To one is given by (διά) the spirit the word of wisdom." 1 Corinthians 12:8.

11. In the same manner it may also be said of the word "in," that Scripture admits its use in the case of God the Father. In the Old Testament it is said through (ἐν) God we shall do valiantly, and, "My praise shall be continually of (ἐν) you;" and again, "In your name will I rejoice." In Paul we read, "In God who created all things," Ephesians 3:9, and, "Paul and Silvanus and Timotheus unto the church of the Thessalonians in God our Father;" 2 Thessalonians 1:1, and "if now at length I might have a prosperous journey by (ἐν) the will of God to come to you;" Romans 1:10, and, "You make your boast of God." Romans 2:17. Instances are indeed too numerous to reckon; but what we want is not so much to exhibit an abundance of evidence as to prove that the conclusions of our opponents are unsound. I shall, therefore, omit any proof of this usage in the case of our Lord and of the Holy Ghost, in that it is notorious. But I cannot forbear to remark that "the wise hearer" will find sufficient proof of the proposition before him by following the method of contraries. For if the difference of language

indicates, as we are told, that the nature has been changed, then let identity of language compel our adversaries to confess with shame that the essence is unchanged.

12. And it is not only in the case of the theology that the use of the terms varies, but whenever one of the terms takes the meaning of the other we find them frequently transferred from the one subject to the other. As, for instance, Adam says, "I have gotten a man through God," meaning to say the same as from God; and in another passage "Moses commanded . . . Israel through the word of the Lord," and, again, "Is not the interpretation through God?" Joseph, discoursing about dreams to the prisoners, instead of saying "from God" says plainly "through God." Inversely Paul uses the term "from whom" instead of "through whom," when he says "made from a woman" (A.V., "of" instead of "through a woman"). Galatians 4:4. And this he has plainly distinguished in another passage, where he says that it is proper to a woman to be made of the man, and to a man to be made through the woman, in the words "For as the woman is from [A.V., of] the man, even so is the man also through [A.V., by] the woman." 1 Corinthians 11:12. Nevertheless in the passage in question the apostle, while illustrating the variety of usage, at the same time corrects obiter the error of those who supposed that the body of the Lord was a spiritual body, and, to show that the God-bearing flesh was formed out of the common lump of human nature, gave precedence to the more emphatic preposition.

The phrase "through a woman" would be likely to give rise to the suspicion of mere transit in the generation, while the phrase "of the woman" would satisfactorily indicate that the nature was shared by the mother and the offspring. The apostle was in no wise contradicting himself, but he showed that the words can without difficulty be interchanged. Since, therefore, the term "from whom" is transferred to the identical subjects in the case of which "through whom" is decided to be properly used, with what consistency can these phrases be invariably distinguished one from the other, in order that fault may be falsely found with true religion?

Chapter 6

Issue joined with those who assert that the Son is not with the Father, but after the Father. Also concerning the equal glory.

13. Our opponents, while they thus artfully and perversely encounter our argument, cannot even have recourse to the plea of ignorance. It is obvious that they are annoyed with us for completing the doxology to the Only Begotten together with the Father, and for not separating the Holy Spirit from the Son. On this account they style us

innovators, revolutionizers, phrase-coiners, and every other possible name of insult. But so far am I from being irritated at their abuse, that, were it not for the fact that their loss causes me "heaviness and continual sorrow," I could almost have said that I was grateful to them for the blasphemy, as though they were agents for providing me with blessing. For "blessed are you," it is said, "when men shall revile you for my sake." Matthew 5:11. The grounds of their indignation are these: The Son, according to them, is not together with the Father, but after the Father. Hence it follows that glory should be ascribed to the Father "through him," but not "with him;" inasmuch as "with him" expresses equality of dignity, while "through him" denotes subordination. They further assert that the Spirit is not to be ranked along with the Father and the Son, but under the Son and the Father; not coordinated, but subordinated; not connumerated, but subnumerated.

With technical terminology of this kind they pervert the simplicity and artlessness of the faith, and thus by their ingenuity, suffering no one else to remain in ignorance, they cut off from themselves the plea that ignorance might demand.

14. Let us first ask them this question: In what sense do they say that the Son is "after the Father;" later in time, or in order, or in dignity? But in time no one is so devoid of sense as to assert that the Maker of the ages holds a second place, when no interval intervenes in the natural conjunction of the Father with the Son. And indeed so far as our conception of human relations goes, it is impossible to think of the Son as being later than the Father, not only from the fact that Father and Son are mutually conceived of in accordance with the relationship subsisting between them, but because posteriority in time is predicated of subjects separated by a less interval from the present, and priority of subjects farther off. For instance, what happened in Noah's time is prior to what happened to the men of Sodom, inasmuch as Noah is more remote from our own day; and, again, the events of the history of the men of Sodom are posterior, because they seem in a sense to approach nearer to our own day. But, in addition to its being a breach of true religion, is it not really the extremest folly to measure the existence of the life which transcends all time and all the ages by its distance from the present? Is it not as though God the Father could be compared with, and be made superior to, God the Son, who exists before the ages, precisely in the same way in which things liable to beginning and corruption are described as prior to one another?

The superior remoteness of the Father is really inconceivable, in that thought and intelligence are wholly impotent to go beyond the generation of the Lord; and St. John has admirably confined the conception within circumscribed boundaries by two words, "In the beginning was the Word." For thought cannot travel outside "was," nor imagination beyond "beginning." Let your thought travel ever so far

Saint Basil

backward you cannot get beyond the "was," and however you may strain and strive to see what is beyond the Son, you will find it impossible to get further than the "beginning." True religion, therefore, thus teaches us to think of the Son together with the Father.

15. If they really conceive of a kind of degradation of the Son in relation to the Father, as though He were in a lower place, so that the Father sits above, and the Son is thrust off to the next seat below, let them confess what they mean. We shall have no more to say. A plain statement of the view will at once expose its absurdity. They who refuse to allow that the Father pervades all things do not so much as maintain the logical sequence of thought in their argument. The faith of the sound is that God fills all things; Ephesians 4:10, but they who divide their up and down between the Father and the Son do not remember even the word of the Prophet: "If I climb up into heaven you are there; if I go down to hell you are there also." Now, to omit all proof of the ignorance of those who predicate place of incorporeal things, what excuse can be found for their attack upon Scripture, shameless as their antagonism is, in the passages "Sit on my right hand" and "Sat down on the right hand of the majesty of God"? The expression "right hand" does not, as they contend, indicate the lower place, but equality of relation; it is not understood physically, in which case there might be something sinister about God, but Scripture puts before us the magnificence of the dignity of the Son by the use of dignified language indicating the seat of honor. It is left then for our opponents to allege that this expression signifies inferiority of rank. Let them learn that "Christ is the power of God and wisdom of God," 1 Corinthians 1:24, and that "He is the image of the invisible God" Colossians 1:15, and "brightness of his glory," Hebrews 1:3, and that "Him has God the Father sealed," John 6:27, by engraving Himself on Him.

Now are we to call these passages, and others like them, throughout the whole of Holy Scripture, proofs of humiliation, or rather public proclamations of the majesty of the Only Begotten, and of the equality of His glory with the Father? We ask them to listen to the Lord Himself, distinctly setting forth the equal dignity of His glory with the Father, in His words, "He that has seen me has seen the Father;" John 14:9, and again, "When the Son comes in the glory of his Father;" Mark 8:38, that they "should honor the Son even as they honor the Father;" John 5:23, and, "We beheld his glory, the glory as of the only begotten of the Father;" John 1:14, and "the only begotten God which is in the bosom of the Father." Of all these passages they take no account, and then assign to the Son the place set apart for His foes. A father's bosom is a fit and becoming seat for a son, but the place of the footstool is for them that have to be forced to fall.

We have only touched cursorily on these proofs, because our

object is to pass on to other points. You at your leisure can put together the items of the evidence, and then contemplate the height of the glory and the preeminence of the power of the Only Begotten. However, to the well-disposed hearer, even these are not insignificant, unless the terms "right hand" and "bosom" be accepted in a physical and derogatory sense, so as at once to circumscribe God in local limits, and invent form, mould, and bodily position, all of which are totally distinct from the idea of the absolute, the infinite, and the incorporeal. There is moreover the fact that what is derogatory in the idea of it is the same in the case both of the Father and the Son; so that whoever repeats these arguments does not take away the dignity of the Son, but does incur the charge of blaspheming the Father; for whatever audacity a man be guilty of against the Son he cannot but transfer to the Father. If he assigns to the Father the upper place by way of precedence, and asserts that the only begotten Son sits below, he will find that to the creature of his imagination attach all the consequent conditions of body. And if these are the imaginations of drunken delusion and frenzied insanity, can it be consistent with true religion for men taught by the Lord himself that "He that honors not the Son honors not the Father" John 5:23, to refuse to worship and glorify with the Father him who in nature, in glory, and in dignity is conjoined with him? What shall we say? What just defense shall we have in the day of the awful universal judgment of all-creation, if, when the Lord clearly announces that He will come "in the glory of his Father;" Matthew 16:27, when Stephen beheld Jesus standing at the right hand of God; Acts 7:55, when Paul testified in the spirit concerning Christ "that he is at the right hand of God;" Romans 8:34, when the Father says, "Sit on my right hand;" when the Holy Spirit bears witness that he has sat down on "the right hand of the majesty" Hebrews 8:1, of God; we attempt to degrade him who shares the honor and the throne, from his condition of equality, to a lower state? Standing and sitting, I apprehend, indicate the fixity and entire stability of the nature, as Baruch, when he wishes to exhibit the immutability and immobility of the Divine mode of existence, says, "For you sit for ever and we perish utterly." Moreover, the place on the right hand indicates in my judgment equality of honor. Rash, then, is the attempt to deprive the Son of participation in the doxology, as though worthy only to be ranked in a lower place of honor.

Chapter 7

Against those who assert that it is not proper for "with whom" to be said of the Son, and that the proper phrase is "through whom."

16. But their contention is that to use the phrase "with him" is altogether strange and unusual, while "through him" is at once most familiar in Holy Scripture, and very common in the language of the brotherhood. What is our answer to this? We say, Blessed are the ears that have not heard you and the hearts that have been kept from the wounds of your words. To you, on the other hand, who are lovers of Christ, I say that the Church recognizes both uses, and deprecates neither as subversive of the other. For whenever we are contemplating the majesty of the nature of the Only Begotten, and the excellence of His dignity, we bear witness that the glory is with the Father; while on the other hand, whenever we bethink us of His bestowal on us of good gifts, and of our access to, and admission into, the household of God, we confess that this grace is effected for us through Him and by Him.

It follows that the one phrase "with whom" is the proper one to be used in the ascription of glory, while the other, "through whom," is specially appropriate in giving of thanks. It is also quite untrue to allege that the phrase "with whom" is unfamiliar in the usage of the devout. All those whose soundness of character leads them to hold the dignity of antiquity to be more honorable than mere new-fangled novelty, and who have preserved the tradition of their fathers unadulterated, alike in town and in country, have employed this phrase. It is, on the contrary, they who are surfeited with the familiar and the customary, and arrogantly assail the old as stale, who welcome innovation, just as in dress your lovers of display always prefer some utter novelty to what is generally worn. So you may even still see that the language of country folk preserves the ancient fashion, while of these, our cunning experts in logomachy, the language bears the brand of the new philosophy.

What our fathers said, the same say we, that the glory of the Father and of the Son is common; wherefore we offer the doxology to the Father with the Son. But we do not rest only on the fact that such is the tradition of the Fathers; for they too followed the sense of Scripture, and started from the evidence which, a few sentences back, I deduced from Scripture and laid before you. For "the brightness" is always thought of with "the glory," "the image" with the archetype, 2 Corinthians 4:4, and the Son always and everywhere together with the Father; nor does even the close connection of the names, much less the nature of the things, admit of separation.

Chapter 8

In how many ways "Through whom" is used; and in what sense "with whom" is more suitable. Explanation of how the Son receives a commandment, and how He is sent.

17. When, then, the apostle "thanks God through Jesus Christ," Romans 1:8, and again says that "through Him" we have "received grace and apostleship for obedience to the faith among all nations," Romans 1:5, or "through Him have access unto this grace wherein we stand and rejoice," Romans 5:2, he sets forth the boons conferred on us by the Son, at one time making the grace of the good gifts pass through from the Father to us, and at another bringing us to the Father through Himself. For by saying "through whom we have received grace and apostleship," Romans 1:5, he declares the supply of the good gifts to proceed from that source; and again in saying "through whom we have had access," Romans 5:2, he sets forth our acceptance and being made "of the household of God" through Christ. Is then the confession of the grace wrought by Him to usward a detraction from His glory? Is it not truer to say that the recital of His benefits is a proper argument for glorifying Him? It is on this account that we have not found Scripture describing the Lord to us by one name, nor even by such terms alone as are indicative of His godhead and majesty. At one time it uses terms descriptive of His nature, for it recognises the "name which is above every name," Philippians 2:9, the name of Son, and speaks of true Son, and only begotten God, and Power of God, and Wisdom, 1 Corinthians 1:24, and Word. Then again, on account of the various manners wherein grace is given to us, which, because of the riches of His goodness, according to his manifold Ephesians 3:10, wisdom, he bestows on them that need, Scripture designates Him by innumerable other titles, calling Him Shepherd, King, Physician, Bridegroom, Way, Door, Fountain, Bread, Axe, and Rock. And these titles do not set forth His nature, but, as I have remarked, the variety of the effectual working which, out of His tender-heartedness to His own creation, according to the peculiar necessity of each, He bestows upon them that need. Them that have fled for refuge to His ruling care, and through patient endurance have mended their wayward ways, He calls "sheep," and confesses Himself to be, to them that hear His voice and refuse to give heed to strange teaching, a "shepherd." For "my sheep," He says, "hear my voice." To them that have now reached a higher stage and stand in need of righteous royalty, He is a King.

And in that, through the straight way of His commandments, He leads men to good actions, and again because He safely shuts in all who through faith in Him betake themselves for shelter to the blessing of the

Saint Basil

higher wisdom, He is a Door.

So He says, "By me if any man enter in, he shall go in and out and shall find pasture." John 10:9. Again, because to the faithful He is a defense strong, unshaken, and harder to break than any bulwark, He is a Rock. Among these titles, it is when He is styled Door, or Way, that the phrase "through Him" is very appropriate and plain. As, however, God and Son, He is glorified with and together with the Father, in that "at, the name of Jesus every knee should bow, of things in heaven, and things in earth, and things under the earth; and that every tongue should confess that Jesus Christ is Lord, to the glory of God the Father." Philippians 2:10-11, Wherefore we use both terms, expressing by the one His own proper dignity, and by the other His grace to usward.

18. For "through Him" comes every succour to our souls, and it is in accordance with each kind of care that an appropriate title has been devised. So when He presents to Himself the blameless soul, not having spot or wrinkle, Ephesians 5:29, like a pure maiden, He is called Bridegroom, but whenever He receives one in sore plight from the devil's evil strokes, healing it in the heavy infirmity of its sins, He is named Physician. And shall this His care for us degrade to meanness our thoughts of Him? Or, on the contrary, shall it smite us with amazement at once at the mighty power and love to man of the Saviour, in that He both endured to suffer with us in our infirmities, and was able to come down to our weakness? For not heaven and earth and the great seas, not the creatures that live in the water and on dry land, not plants, and stars, and air, and seasons, not the vast variety in the order of the universe, so well sets forth the excellency of His might as that God, being incomprehensible, should have been able, impassibly, through flesh, to have come into close conflict with death, to the end that by His own suffering He might give us the boon of freedom from suffering. The apostle, it is true, says, "In all these things we are more than conquerors through him that loved us." Romans 8:37, But in a phrase of this kind there is no suggestion of any lowly and subordinate ministry, but rather of the succour rendered "in the power of his might." Ephesians 6:10, For He Himself has bound the strong man and spoiled his goods, that is, us men, whom our enemy had abused in every evil activity, and made "vessels meet for the Master's use" 2 Timothy 2:21, us who have been perfected for every work through the making ready of that part of us which is in our own control. Thus we have had our approach to the Father through Him, being translated from "the power of darkness to be partakers of the inheritance of the saints in light." Colossians 1:12-13, We must not, however, regard the economy through the Son as a compulsory and subordinate ministration resulting from the low estate of a slave, but rather the voluntary solicitude working effectually for His own creation in goodness and in pity, according to the will of God the Father. For we shall be consistent

with true religion if in all that was and is from time to time perfected by Him, we both bear witness to the perfection of His power, and in no case put it asunder from the Father's will. For instance, whenever the Lord is called the Way, we are carried on to a higher meaning, and not to that which is derived from the vulgar sense of the word. We understand by Way that advance to perfection which is made stage by stage, and in regular order, through the works of righteousness and "the illumination of knowledge;" ever longing after what is before, and reaching forth unto those things which remain, until we shall have reached the blessed end, the knowledge of God, which the Lord through Himself bestows on them that have trusted in Him. For our Lord is an essentially good Way, where erring and straying are unknown, to that which is essentially good, to the Father. For "no one," He says, comes to the Father but ["by" A.V.] through me. John 14:6 Such is our way up to God "through the Son."

19. It will follow that we should next in order point out the character of the provision of blessings bestowed on us by the Father "through him." Inasmuch as all created nature, both this visible world and all that is conceived of in the mind, cannot hold together without the care and providence of God, the Creator Word, the Only begotten God, apportioning His succour according to the measure of the needs of each, distributes mercies various and manifold on account of the many kinds and characters of the recipients of His bounty, but appropriate to the necessities of individual requirements. Those that are confined in the darkness of ignorance He enlightens: for this reason He is true Light. John 1:9. Portioning requital in accordance with the desert of deeds, He judges: for this reason He is righteous Judge. 2 Timothy 4:8, "For the Father judges no man, but has committed all judgment to the Son." John 5:22. Those that have lapsed from the lofty height of life into sin He raises from their fall: for this reason He is Resurrection. John 11:25. Effectually working by the touch of His power and the will of His goodness He does all things. He shepherds; He enlightens; He nourishes; He heals; He guides; He raises up; He calls into being things that were not; He upholds what has been created. Thus the good things that come from God reach us "through the Son," who works in each case with greater speed than speech can utter. For not lightnings, not light's course in air, is so swift; not eyes' sharp turn, not the movements of our very thought. Nay, by the divine energy is each one of these in speed further surpassed than is the slowest of all living creatures outdone in motion by birds, or even winds, or the rush of the heavenly bodies: or, not to mention these, by our very thought itself. For what extent of time is needed by Him who "upholds all things by the word of His power," Hebrews 1:3, and works not by bodily agency, nor requires the help of hands to form and fashion, but holds in obedient following and unforced consent the nature of all things that

Saint Basil

are? So as Judith says, "You have thought, and what things you determined were ready at hand." On the other hand, and lest we should ever be drawn away by the greatness of the works wrought to imagine that the Lord is without beginning, what says the Self-Existent? "I live through [by, A.V.] the Father," John 6:57, and the power of God; "The Son has power [can, A.V.] to do nothing of himself." John 5:19, And the self-complete Wisdom? I received "a commandment what I should say and what I should speak." John 12:49, Through all these words He is guiding us to the knowledge of the Father, and referring our wonder at all that is brought into existence to Him, to the end that "through Him" we may know the Father. For the Father is not regarded from the difference of the operations, by the exhibition of a separate and peculiar energy; for whatsoever things He sees the Father doing, "these also does the Son likewise;" John 5:19, but He enjoys our wonder at all that comes to pass out of the glory which comes to Him from the Only Begotten, rejoicing in the Doer Himself as well as in the greatness of the deeds, and exalted by all who acknowledge Him as Father of our Lord Jesus Christ, "through whom [by whom, A.V.] are all things, and for whom are all things." Wherefore, says the Lord, "All mine are yours," John 17:10, as though the sovereignty over created things were conferred on Him, and "Yours are mine," as though the creating Cause came thence to Him. We are not to suppose that He used assistance in His action, or yet was entrusted with the ministry of each individual work by detailed commission, a condition distinctly menial and quite inadequate to the divine dignity. Rather was the Word full of His Father's excellences; He shines forth from the Father, and does all things according to the likeness of Him that begot Him. For if in essence He is without variation, so also is He without variation in power. And of those whose power is equal, the operation also is in all ways equal. And Christ is the power of God, and the wisdom of God. 1 Corinthians 1:24. And so "all things are made through [by, A.V.] him," John 1:3, and "all things were created through [by, A.V.] him and for him," Colossians 1:16, not in the discharge of any slavish service, but in the fulfillment of the Father's will as Creator.

20. When then He says, "I have not spoken of myself," John 12:49, and again, "As the Father said to me, so I speak," John 12:50, and "The word which you hear is not mine, but [the Father's] which sent me," John 14:24, and in another place, "As the Father gave me commandment, even so I do," John 14:31, it is not because He lacks deliberate purpose or power of initiation, nor yet because He has to wait for the preconcerted key-note, that he employs language of this kind. His object is to make it plain that His own will is connected in indissoluble union with the Father. Do not then let us understand by what is called a "commandment" a peremptory mandate delivered by organs of speech, and giving orders to the Son, as to a subordinate,

concerning what He ought to do. Let us rather, in a sense befitting the Godhead, perceive a transmission of will, like the reflection of an object in a mirror, passing without note of time from Father to Son. "For the Father loves the Son and shows him all things," John 5:20, so that "all things that the Father has" belong to the Son, not gradually accruing to Him little by little, but with Him all together and at once. Among men, the workman who has been thoroughly taught his craft, and, through long training, has sure and established experience in it, is able, in accordance with the scientific methods which now he has in store, to work for the future by himself. And are we to suppose that the wisdom of God, the Maker of all creation, He who is eternally perfect, who is wise, without a teacher, the Power of God, "in whom are hid all the treasures of wisdom and knowledge," needs piecemeal instruction to mark out the manner and measure of His operations? I presume that in the vanity of your calculations, you mean to open a school; you will make the one take His seat in the teacher's place, and the other stand by in a scholar's ignorance, gradually learning wisdom and advancing to perfection, by lessons given Him bit by bit. Hence, if you have sense to abide by what logically follows, you will find the Son being eternally taught, nor yet ever able to reach the end of perfection, inasmuch as the wisdom of the Father is infinite, and the end of the infinite is beyond apprehension. It results that whoever refuses to grant that the Son has all things from the beginning will never grant that He will reach perfection. But I am ashamed at the degraded conception to which, by the course of the argument, I have been brought down. Let us therefore revert to the loftier themes of our discussion.

21. He that has seen me has seen the Father; John 14:9, not the express image, nor yet the form, for the divine nature does not admit of combination; but the goodness of the will, which, being concurrent with the essence, is beheld as like and equal, or rather the same, in the Father as in the Son.

What then is meant by "became subject"? Philippians 2:8. What by "delivered him up for us all"? Romans 8:32. It is meant that the Son has it of the Father that He works in goodness on behalf of men. But you must hear too the words, "Christ has redeemed us from the curse of the law;" Galatians 3:13, and "while we were yet sinners, Christ died for us." Romans 5:8.

Give careful heed, too, to the words of the Lord, and note how, whenever He instructs us about His Father, He is in the habit of using terms of personal authority, saying, "I will; be clean;" Matthew 8:3, and "Peace, be still;" Mark 4:39, and "But I say unto you;" and "Thou dumb and deaf spirit, I charge you;" Mark 9:25, and all other expressions of the same kind, in order that by these we may recognize our Master and Maker, and by the former may be taught the Father of our Master and Creator. Thus on all sides is demonstrated the true doctrine that the fact that the Father creates through the Son neither constitutes the creation of the Father imperfect nor exhibits the active energy of the Son as feeble, but indicates the unity of the will; so the expression "through whom" contains a confession of an antecedent Cause, and is not adopted in objection to the efficient Cause.

Chapter 9

Definitive conceptions about the Spirit which conform to the teaching of the Scriptures.

22. Let us now investigate what are our common conceptions concerning the Spirit, as well those which have been gathered by us from Holy Scripture concerning It as those which we have received from the unwritten tradition of the Fathers. First of all we ask, who on hearing the titles of the Spirit is not lifted up in soul, who does not raise his conception to the supreme nature? It is called "Spirit of God," "Spirit of truth which proceeds from the Father," John 15:26, "right Spirit," "a leading Spirit." Its proper and peculiar title is "Holy Spirit;" which is a name specially appropriate to everything that is incorporeal, purely immaterial, and indivisible. So our Lord, when teaching the woman who thought God to be an object of local worship that the incorporeal is incomprehensible, said "God is a spirit." John 4:24. On our hearing, then, of a spirit, it is impossible to form the idea of a nature circumscribed, subject to change and variation, or at all like the creature. We are compelled to advance in our conceptions to the highest, and to think of an intelligent essence, in power infinite, in magnitude unlimited, unmeasured by times or ages, generous of Its good gifts, to whom turn all things needing sanctification, after whom reach all things that live in virtue, as being watered by Its inspiration and helped on toward their natural and proper end; perfecting all other things, but Itself in nothing lacking; living not as needing restoration, but as Supplier of life; not growing by additions; but straightway full, self-established, omnipresent, origin of sanctification, light perceptible to the mind, supplying, as it were, through Itself, illumination to every faculty in the search for truth; by nature unapproachable, apprehended by reason of goodness, filling all things with Its power, but communicated only to the worthy; not shared in one measure, but distributing Its energy according to "the proportion of faith;" Romans 12:6, in essence simple, in powers various, wholly present in each and being wholly everywhere; impassively divided, shared without loss of ceasing to be entire, after the likeness of the sunbeam, whose kindly light falls on him who enjoys it as though it shone for him alone, yet illumines land and sea and mingles with the air. So, too, is the Spirit to every one who receives it, as though given to him alone, and yet It

sends forth grace sufficient and full for all mankind, and is enjoyed by all who share It, according to the capacity, not of Its power, but of their nature.

23. Now the Spirit is not brought into intimate association with the soul by local approximation. How indeed could there be a corporeal approach to the incorporeal? This association results from the withdrawal of the passions which, coming afterwards gradually on the soul from its friendship to the flesh, have alienated it from its close relationship with God. Only then after a man is purified from the shame whose stain he took through his wickedness, and has come back again to his natural beauty, and as it were cleaning the Royal Image and restoring its ancient form, only thus is it possible for him to draw near to the Paraclete. And He, like the sun, will by the aid of your purified eye show you in Himself the image of the invisible, and in the blessed spectacle of the image you shall behold the unspeakable beauty of the archetype. Through His aid hearts are lifted up, the weak are held by the hand, and they who are advancing are brought to perfection. Shining upon those that are cleansed from every spot, He makes them spiritual by fellowship with Himself. Just as when a sunbeam falls on bright and transparent bodies, they themselves become brilliant too, and shed forth a fresh brightness from themselves, so souls wherein the Spirit dwells, illuminated by the Spirit, themselves become spiritual, and send forth their grace to others. Hence comes foreknowledge of the future, understanding of mysteries, apprehension of what is hidden, distribution of good gifts, the heavenly citizenship, a place in the chorus of angels, joy without end, abiding in God, the being made like to God, and, highest of all, the being made God. Such, then, to instance a few out of many, are the conceptions concerning the Holy Spirit, which we have been taught to hold concerning His greatness, His dignity, and His operations, by the oracles of the Spirit themselves.

Chapter 10

Against those who say that it is not right to rank the Holy Spirit with the Father and the Son.

24. But we must proceed to attack our opponents, in the endeavour to confute those "oppositions" advanced against us which are derived from "knowledge falsely so-called."

It is not permissible, they assert, for the Holy Spirit to be ranked with the Father and Son, on account of the difference of His nature and the inferiority of His dignity. Against them it is right to reply in the words of the apostles, "We ought to obey God rather than men." Acts 5:29.

For if our Lord, when enjoining the baptism of salvation, charged

His disciples to baptize all nations in the name "of the Father and of the Son and of the Holy Ghost," Matthew 28:19, not disdaining fellowship with Him, and these men allege that we must not rank Him with the Father and the Son, is it not clear that they openly withstand the commandment of God? If they deny that coordination of this kind is declaratory of any fellowship and conjunction, let them tell us why it behooves us to hold this opinion, and what more intimate mode of conjunction they have.

If the Lord did not indeed conjoin the Spirit with the Father and Himself in baptism, do not let them lay the blame of conjunction upon us, for we neither hold nor say anything different. If on the contrary the Spirit is there conjoined with the Father and the Son, and no one is so shameless as to say anything else, then let them not lay blame on us for following the words of Scripture.

25. But all the apparatus of war has been got ready against us; every intellectual missile is aimed at us; and now blasphemers' tongues shoot and hit and hit again, yet harder than Stephen of old was smitten by the killers of the Christ. And do not let them succeed in concealing the fact that, while an attack on us serves for a pretext for the war, the real aim of these proceedings is higher. It is against us, they say, that they are preparing their engines and their snares; against us that they are shouting to one another, according to each one's strength or cunning, to come on. But the object of attack is faith. The one aim of the whole band of opponents and enemies of "sound doctrine" 1 Timothy 1:10, is to shake down the foundation of the faith of Christ by levelling apostolic tradition with the ground, and utterly destroying it. So like the debtors—of course bona fide debtors—they clamour for written proof, and reject as worthless the unwritten tradition of the Fathers. But we will not slacken in our defense of the truth. We will not cowardly abandon the cause. The Lord has delivered to us as a necessary and saving doctrine that the Holy Spirit is to be ranked with the Father. Our opponents think differently, and see fit to divide and rend asunder, and relegate Him to the nature of a ministering spirit. Is it not then indisputable that they make their own blasphemy more authoritative than the law prescribed by the Lord? Come, then, set aside mere contention. Let us consider the points before us, as follows:

26. Whence is it that we are Christians? Through our faith, would be the universal answer. And in what way are we saved? Plainly because we were regenerate through the grace given in our baptism. How else could we be? And after recognising that this salvation is established through the Father and the Son and the Holy Ghost, shall we fling away "that form of doctrine" Romans 6:17, which we received? Would it not rather be ground for great groaning if we are found now further off from our salvation "than when we first believed," and deny now what we then received? Whether a man have departed

this life without baptism, or have received a baptism lacking in some of the requirements of the tradition, his loss is equal. And whoever does not always and everywhere keep to and hold fast as a sure protection the confession which we recorded at our first admission, when, being delivered "from the idols," we came "to the living God," 1 Thessalonians 1:9, constitutes himself a "stranger" from the "promises" Ephesians 2:12, of God, fighting against his own handwriting, which he put on record when he professed the faith. For if to me my baptism was the beginning of life, and that day of regeneration the first of days, it is plain that the utterance uttered in the grace of adoption was the most honorable of all. Can I then, perverted by these men's seductive words, abandon the tradition which guided me to the light, which bestowed on me the boon of the knowledge of God, whereby I, so long a foe by reason of sin, was made a child of God? But, for myself, I pray that with this confession I may depart hence to the Lord, and them I charge to preserve the faith secure until the day of Christ, and to keep the Spirit undivided from the Father and the Son, preserving, both in the confession of faith and in the doxology, the doctrine taught them at their baptism.

Chapter 11

That they who deny the Spirit are transgressors.

27. "Who has woe? Who has sorrow?" Proverbs 23:29. For whom is distress and darkness? For whom eternal doom? Is it not for the transgressors? For them that deny the faith? And what is the proof of their denial? Is it not that they have set at naught their own confessions? And when and what did they confess? Belief in the Father and in the Son and in the Holy Ghost, when they renounced the devil and his angels, and uttered those saving words. What fit title then for them has been discovered, for the children of light to use? Are they not addressed as transgressors, as having violated the covenant of their salvation? What am I to call the denial of God? What the denial of Christ? What but transgressions? And to him who denies the Spirit, what title do you wish me to apply? Must it not be the same, inasmuch as he has broken his covenant with God? And when the confession of faith in Him secures the blessing of true religion. and its denial subjects men to the doom of godlessness, is it not a fearful thing for them to set the confession at naught, not through fear of fire, or sword, or cross, or scourge, or wheel, or rack, but merely led astray by the sophistry and seductions of the pneumatomachi? I testify to every man who is confessing Christ and denying God, that Christ will profit him nothing; to every man that calls upon God but rejects the Son, that his faith is vain; to every man that sets aside the Spirit, that his faith in the Father

and the Son will be useless, for he cannot even hold it without the presence of the Spirit. For he who does not believe the Spirit does not believe in the Son, and he who has not believed in the Son does not believe in the Father. For none "can say that Jesus is the Lord but by the Holy Ghost," 1 Corinthians 12:3, and "No man has seen God at any time, but the only begotten God which is in the bosom of the Father, he has declared him."

Such an one has neither part nor lot in the true worship; for it is impossible to worship the Son, save by the Holy Ghost; impossible to call upon the Father, save by the Spirit of adoption.

Chapter 12

Against those who assert that the baptism in the name of the Father alone is sufficient.

28. Let no one be misled by the fact of the apostle's frequently omitting the name of the Father and of the Holy Spirit when making mention of baptism, or on this account imagine that the invocation of the names is not observed. "As many of you," he says, "as were baptized into Christ have put on Christ;" and again, "As many of you as were baptized into Christ were baptized into his death." For the naming of Christ is the confession of the whole, showing forth as it does the God who gave, the Son who received, and the Spirit who is, the unction. So we have learned from Peter, in the Acts, of "Jesus of Nazareth whom God anointed with the Holy Ghost;" Acts 10:38, and in Isaiah, "The Spirit of the Lord is upon me, because the Lord has anointed me;" Isaiah 60:1, and the Psalmist, "Therefore God, even your God, has anointed you with the oil of gladness above your fellows." Scripture, however, in the case of baptism, sometimes plainly mentions the Spirit alone.

"For into one Spirit," it says, "we were all baptized in one body." And in harmony with this are the passages: "You shall be baptized with the Holy Ghost," Acts 1:5, and "He shall baptize you with the Holy Ghost." Luke 3:16. But no one on this account would be justified in calling that baptism a perfect baptism wherein only the name of the Spirit was invoked. For the tradition that has been given us by the quickening grace must remain for ever inviolate. He who redeemed our life from destruction gave us power of renewal, whereof the cause is ineffable and hidden in mystery, but bringing great salvation to our souls, so that to add or to take away anything involves manifestly a falling away from the life everlasting. If then in baptism the separation of the Spirit from the Father and the Son is perilous to the baptizer, and of no advantage to the baptized, how can the rending asunder of the Spirit from Father and from Son be safe for us? Faith and baptism are two kindred and inseparable ways of salvation: faith is perfected through baptism, baptism is established through faith, and both are completed by the same names. For as we believe in the Father and the Son and the Holy Ghost, so are we also baptized in the name of the Father and of the Son and of the Holy Ghost; first comes the confession, introducing us to salvation, and baptism follows, setting the seal upon our assent.

Chapter 13

Statement of the reason why in the writings of Paul the angels are associated with the Father and the Son.

29. It is, however, objected that other beings which are enumerated with the Father and the Son are certainly not always glorified together with them. The apostle, for instance, in his charge to Timothy, associates the angels with them in the words, "I charge you before God and the Lord Jesus Christ and the elect angels." 1 Timothy 5:21. We are not for alienating the angels from the rest of creation, and yet, it is argued, we do not allow of their being reckoned with the Father and the Son. To this I reply, although the argument, so obviously absurd is it, does not really deserve a reply, that possibly before a mild and gentle judge, and especially before One who by His leniency to those arraigned before Him demonstrates the unimpeachable equity of His decisions, one might be willing to offer as witness even a fellow-slave; but for a slave to be made free and called a son of God and quickened from death can only be brought about by Him who has acquired natural kinship with us, and has been changed from the rank of a slave. For how can we be made kin with God by one who is an alien? How can we be freed by one who is himself under the yoke of slavery? It follows that the mention of the Spirit and that of angels are not made under like conditions. The Spirit is called on as Lord of life, and the angels as allies of their fellow-slaves and faithful witnesses of the truth. It is customary for the saints to deliver the commandments of God in the presence of witnesses, as also the apostle himself says to Timothy, "The things which you have heard of me among many witnesses, the same commit thou to faithful men;" 2 Timothy 2:2, and now he calls the angels to witness, for he knows that angels shall be present with the Lord when He shall come in the glory of His Father to judge the world in righteousness. For He says, "Whoever shall confess me before men, him shall the Son of Man also confess before the angels of God, but he that denies Me before men shall be denied before the angels of God;" Luke 12:8-9, and Paul in another place says, "When the Lord Jesus shall be revealed from heaven with his angels." 2 Thessalonians 1:7. Thus he already testifies before the angels, preparing good proofs for

himself at the great tribunal.

30. And not only Paul, but generally all those to whom is committed any ministry of the word, never cease from testifying, but call heaven and earth to witness on the ground that now every deed that is done is done within them, and that in the examination of all the actions of life they will be present with the judged. So it is said, "He shall call to the heavens above and to earth, that he may judge his people." And so Moses when about to deliver his oracles to the people says, "I call heaven and earth to witness this day;" Deuteronomy 4:26, and again in his song he says, "Give ear, O you heavens, and I will speak, and hear, O earth, the words of my mouth;" Deuteronomy 32:1, and Isaiah, "Hear, O heavens, and give ear, O earth;" Isaiah 1:2, and Jeremiah describes astonishment in heaven at the tidings of the unholy deeds of the people: "The heaven was astonished at this, and was horribly afraid, because my people committed two evils." And so the apostle, knowing the angels to be set over men as tutors and guardians, calls them to witness. Moreover, Joshua, the son of Nun, even set up a stone as witness of his words (already a heap somewhere had been called a witness by Jacob), Genesis 31:47, for he says, "Behold this stone shall be a witness unto you this day to the end of days, when you lie to the Lord our God," perhaps believing that by God's power even the stones would speak to the conviction of the transgressors; or, if not, that at least each man's conscience would be wounded by the force of the reminder. In this manner they who have been entrusted with the stewardship of souls provide witnesses, whatever they may be, so as to produce them at some future day. But the Spirit is ranked together with God, not on account of the emergency of the moment, but on account of the natural fellowship; is not dragged in by us, but invited by the Lord.

Chapter 14

Objection that some were baptized unto Moses and believed in him, and an answer to it; with remarks upon types.

31. But even if some are baptized unto the Spirit, it is not, it is urged, on this account right for the Spirit to be ranked with God. Some "were baptized unto Moses in the cloud and in the sea." 1 Corinthians 10:2. And it is admitted that faith even before now has been put in men; for "The people believed God and his servant Moses." Why then, it is asked, do we, on account of faith and of baptism, exalt and magnify the Holy Spirit so far above creation, when there is evidence that the same things have before now been said of men? What, then, shall we reply? Our answer is that the faith in the Spirit is the same as the faith in the Father and the Son; and in like manner, too, the baptism. But the faith

in Moses and in the cloud is, as it were, in a shadow and type. The nature of the divine is very frequently represented by the rough and shadowy outlines of the types; but because divine things are prefigured by small and human things, it is obvious that we must not therefore conclude the divine nature to be small. The type is an exhibition of things expected, and gives an imitative anticipation of the future. So Adam was a type of "Him that was to come." Romans 5:14. Typically, "That rock was Christ;" 1 Corinthians 10:4, and the water a type of the living power of the word; as He says, "If any man thirst, let him come unto me and drink." John 7:37. The manna is a type of the living bread that came down from heaven; John 6:49, 51, and the serpent on the standard, of the passion of salvation accomplished by means of the cross, wherefore they who even looked thereon were preserved. So in like manner, the history of the exodus of Israel is recorded to show forth those who are being saved through baptism. For the firstborn of the Israelites were preserved, like the bodies of the baptized, by the giving of grace to them that were marked with blood. For the blood of the sheep is a type of the blood of Christ; and the firstborn, a type of the first-formed. And inasmuch as the first-formed of necessity exists in us, and, in sequence of succession, is transmitted till the end, it follows that "in Adam" we "all die," 1 Corinthians 15:22, and that "death reigned," Romans 5:17, until the fulfilling of the law and the coming of Christ. And the firstborn were preserved by God from being touched by the destroyer, to show that we who were made alive in Christ no longer die in Adam. The sea and the cloud for the time being led on through amazement to faith, but for the time to come they typically prefigured the grace to be. "Who is wise and he shall understand these things?" Hosea 14:9—how the sea is typically a baptism bringing about the departure of Pharaoh, in like manner as this washing causes the departure of the tyranny of the devil. The sea slew the enemy in itself: and in baptism too dies our enmity towards God. From the sea the people came out unharmed: we too, as it were, alive from the dead, step up from the water "saved" by the "grace" of Him who called us. Ephesians 2:5. And the cloud is a shadow of the gift of the Spirit, who cools the flame of our passions by the "mortification" of our "members." Colossians 3:5.

32. What then? Because they were typically baptized unto Moses, is the grace of baptism therefore small? Were it so, and if we were in each case to prejudice the dignity of our privileges by comparing them with their types, not even one of these privileges could be reckoned great; then not the love of God, who gave His only begotten Son for our sins, would be great and extraordinary, because Abraham did not spare his own son; then even the passion of the Lord would not be glorious, because a sheep typified the offering instead of Isaac; then the descent into hell was not fearful, because Jonah had previously typified the

Saint Basil 33

death in three days and three nights. The same prejudicial comparison is made also in the case of baptism by all who judge of the reality by the shadow, and, comparing the typified with the type, attempt by means of Moses and the sea to disparage at once the whole dispensation of the Gospel. What remission of sins, what renewal of life, is there in the sea? What spiritual gift is there through Moses? What dying of sins is there? Those men did not die with Christ; wherefore they were not raised with Him. They did not "bear the image of the heavenly;" 1 Corinthians 15:49, they did "bear about in the body the dying of Jesus;" 2 Corinthians 4:10, they did not "put off the old man;" they did not "put on the new man which is renewed in knowledge after the image of Him which created him." Colossians 3:9-10. Why then do you compare baptisms which have only the name in common, while the distinction between the things themselves is as great as might be that of dream and reality, that of shadow and figures with substantial existence?

33. But belief in Moses not only does not show our belief in the Spirit to be worthless, but, if we adopt our opponents' line of argument, it rather weakens our confession in the God of the universe. "The people," it is written, "believed the Lord and his servant Moses." Exodus 14:31. Moses then is joined with God, not with the Spirit; and he was a type not of the Spirit, but of Christ. For at that time in the ministry of the law, he by means of himself typified "the Mediator between God and men." 1 Timothy 2:5. Moses, when mediating for the people in things pertaining to God, was not a minister of the Spirit; for the law was given, "ordained by angels in the hand of a mediator," Galatians 3:19, namely Moses, in accordance with the summons of the people, "Speak thou with us,... but let not God speak with us." Exodus 20:19. Thus faith in Moses is referred to the Lord, the Mediator between God and men, who said, "Had ye believed Moses, you would have believed me." John 5:46. Is then our faith in the Lord a trifle, because it was signified beforehand through Moses? So then, even if men were baptized unto Moses, it does not follow that the grace given of the Spirit in baptism is small. I may point out, too, that it is usual in Scripture to say Moses and the law, as in the passage, "They have Moses and the prophets." Luke 16:29. When therefore it is meant to speak of the baptism of the law, the words are, "They were baptized unto Moses." 1 Corinthians 10:2. Why then do these calumniators of the truth, by means of the shadow and the types, endeavour to bring contempt and ridicule on the "rejoicing" of our "hope," Hebrews 3:6, and the rich gift of our God and Saviour, who through regeneration renews our youth like the eagle's? Surely it is altogether childish, and like a babe who must needs be fed on milk, to be ignorant of the great mystery of our salvation; inasmuch as, in accordance with the gradual progress of our education, while being brought to perfection in our

training for godliness, we were first taught elementary and easier lessons, suited to our intelligence, while the Dispenser of our lots was ever leading us up, by gradually accustoming us, like eyes brought up in the dark, to the great light of truth. For He spares our weakness, and in the depth of the riches Romans 11:33, of His wisdom, and the inscrutable judgments of His intelligence, used this gentle treatment, fitted for our needs, gradually accustoming us to see first the shadows of objects, and to look at the sun in water, to save us from dashing against the spectacle of pure unadulterated light, and being blinded. Just so the Law, having a shadow of things to come, and the typical teaching of the prophets, which is a dark utterance of the truth, have been devised means to train the eyes of the heart, in that hence the transition to the wisdom hidden in mystery, 1 Corinthians 2:7, will be made easy. Enough so far concerning types; nor indeed would it be possible to linger longer on this topic, or the incidental discussion would become many times bulkier than the main argument.

Chapter 15

Reply to the suggested objection that we are baptized "into water." Also concerning baptism.

34. What more? Verily, our opponents are well equipped with arguments. We are baptized, they urge, into water, and of course we shall not honor the water above all creation, or give it a share of the honor of the Father and of the Son. The arguments of these men are such as might be expected from angry disputants, leaving no means untried in their attack on him who has offended them, because their reason is clouded over by their feelings. We will not, however, shrink from the discussion even of these points. If we do not teach the ignorant, at least we shall not turn away before evil doers. But let us for a moment retrace our steps.

35. The dispensation of our God and Saviour concerning man is a recall from the fall and a return from the alienation caused by disobedience to close communion with God. This is the reason for the sojourn of Christ in the flesh, the pattern life described in the Gospels, the sufferings, the cross, the tomb, the resurrection; so that the man who is being saved through imitation of Christ receives that old adoption. For perfection of life the imitation of Christ is necessary, not only in the example of gentleness, lowliness, and long suffering set us in His life, but also of His actual death. So Paul, the imitator of Christ, says, "being made conformable unto his death; if by any means I might attain unto the resurrection of the dead." Philippians 3:10-11. How then are we made in the likeness of His death? Romans 6:4-5. In that we were buried with Him by baptism. What then is the manner of the

burial? And what is the advantage resulting from the imitation? First of all, it is necessary that the continuity of the old life be cut. And this is impossible less a man be born again, according to the Lord's word; John 3:3, for the regeneration, as indeed the name shows, is a beginning of a second life. So before beginning the second, it is necessary to put an end to the first. For just as in the case of runners who turn and take the second course, a kind of halt and pause intervenes between the movements in the opposite direction, so also in making a change in lives it seemed necessary for death to come as mediator between the two, ending all that goes before, and beginning all that comes after. How then do we achieve the descent into hell? By imitating, through baptism, the burial of Christ. For the bodies of the baptized are, as it were, buried in the water. Baptism then symbolically signifies the putting off of the works of the flesh; as the apostle says, you were "circumcised with the circumcision made without hands, in putting off the body of the sins of the flesh by the circumcision of Christ; buried with him in baptism." Colossians 2:11-12. And there is, as it were, a cleansing of the soul from the filth that has grown on it from the carnal mind, as it is written, "You shall wash me, and I shall be whiter than snow." On this account we do not, as is the fashion of the Jews, wash ourselves at each defilement, but own the baptism of salvation to be one. For there the death on behalf of the world is one, and one the resurrection of the dead, whereof baptism is a type. For this cause the Lord, who is the Dispenser of our life, gave us the covenant of baptism, containing a type of life and death, for the water fulfils the image of death, and the Spirit gives us the earnest of life. Hence it follows that the answer to our question why the water was associated with the Spirit is clear: the reason is because in baptism two ends were proposed; on the one hand, the destroying of the body of sin, that it may never bear fruit unto death; on the other hand, our living unto the Spirit, and having our fruit in holiness; the water receiving the body as in a tomb figures death, while the Spirit pours in the quickening power, renewing our souls from the deadness of sin unto their original life. This then is what it is to be born again of water and of the Spirit, the being made dead being effected in the water, while our life is wrought in us through the Spirit. In three immersions, then, and with three invocations, the great mystery of baptism is performed, to the end that the type of death may be fully figured, and that by the tradition of the divine knowledge the baptized may have their souls enlightened. It follows that if there is any grace in the water, it is not of the nature of the water, but of the presence of the Spirit. For baptism is "not the putting away of the filth of the flesh, but the answer of a good conscience towards God." 1 Peter 3:21. So in training us for the life that follows on the resurrection the Lord sets out all the manner of life required by the Gospel, laying down for us the law of gentleness, of endurance of wrong, of freedom from the defilement that comes of the love of pleasure, and from covetousness, to the end that we may of set purpose win beforehand and achieve all that the life to come of its inherent nature possesses. If therefore any one in attempting a definition were to describe the gospel as a forecast of the life that follows on the resurrection, he would not seem to me to go beyond what is meet and right. Let us now return to our main topic.

36. Through the Holy Spirit comes our restoration to paradise, our ascension into the kingdom of heaven, our return to the adoption of sons, our liberty to call God our Father, our being made partakers of the grace of Christ, our being called children of light, our sharing in eternal glory, and, in a word, our being brought into a state of all "fullness of blessing," Romans 15:29, both in this world and in the world to come, of all the good gifts that are in store for us, by promise hereof, through faith, beholding the reflection of their grace as though they were already present, we await the full enjoyment. If such is the earnest, what the perfection? If such the first fruits, what the complete fulfillment? Furthermore, from this too may be apprehended the difference between the grace that comes from the Spirit and the baptism by water: in that John indeed baptized with water, but our Lord Jesus Christ by the Holy Ghost. "I indeed," he says, "baptize you with water unto repentance; but he that comes after me is mightier than I, whose shoes I am not worthy to bear: he shall baptize you with the Holy Ghost and with fire." Matthew 3:11. Here He calls the trial at the judgment the baptism of fire, as the apostle says, "The fire shall try every man's work, of what sort it is." 1 Corinthians 3:13. And again, "The day shall declare it, because it shall be revealed by fire." 1 Corinthians 3:13. And ere now there have been some who in their championship of true religion have undergone the death for Christ's sake, not in mere similitude, but in actual fact, and so have needed none of the outward signs of water for their salvation, because they were baptized in their own blood. Thus I write not to disparage the baptism by water, but to overthrow the arguments of those who exalt themselves against the Spirit; who confound things that are distinct from one another, and compare those which admit of no comparison.

Chapter 16

That the Holy Spirit is in every conception separable from the Father and the Son, alike in the creation of perceptible objects, in the dispensation of human affairs, and in the judgment to come.

37. Let us then revert to the point raised from the outset, that in all things the Holy Spirit is inseparable and wholly incapable of being parted from the Father and the Son. St. Paul, in the passage about the

gift of tongues, writes to the Corinthians, "If you all prophesy and there come in one that believes not, or one unlearned, he is convinced of all, he is judged of all; and thus are the secrets of the heart made manifest; and so falling down on his face he will worship God and report that God is in you of a truth." 1 Corinthians 14:24-25. If then God is known to be in the prophets by the prophesying that is acting according to the distribution of the gifts of the Spirit, let our adversaries consider what kind of place they will attribute to the Holy Spirit. Let them say whether it is more proper to rank Him with God or to thrust Him forth to the place of the creature. Peter's words to Sapphira, "How is it that you have agreed together to tempt the Spirit of the Lord? You have not lied unto men, but unto God," show that sins against the Holy Spirit and against God are the same; and thus you might learn that in every operation the Spirit is closely conjoined with, and inseparable from, the Father and the Son. God works the differences of operations, and the Lord the diversities of administrations, but all the while the Holy Spirit is present too of His own will, dispensing distribution of the gifts according to each recipient's worth. For, it is said, "there are diversities of gifts, but the same Spirit; and differences of administrations, but the same Lord; and there are diversities of operations, but it is the same God which works all in all." "But all these," it is said, "works that one and the self-same Spirit, dividing to every man severally as He will." 1 Corinthians 12:11. It must not however be supposed because in this passage the apostle names in the first place the Spirit, in the second the Son, and in the third God the Father, that therefore their rank is reversed. The apostle has only started in accordance with our habits of thought; for when we receive gifts, the first that occurs to us is the distributer, next we think of the sender, and then we lift our thoughts to the fountain and cause of the boons.

38. Moreover, from the things created at the beginning may be learned the fellowship of the Spirit with the Father and the Son. The pure, intelligent, and super mundane powers are and are styled holy, because they have their holiness of the grace given by the Holy Spirit. Accordingly the mode of the creation of the heavenly powers is passed over in Silence, for the historian of the cosmogony has revealed to us only the creation of things perceptible by sense. But do thou, who hast power from the things that are seen to form an analogy of the unseen, glorify the Maker by whom all things were made, visible and invisible, principalities and powers, authorities, thrones, and dominions, and all other reasonable natures whom we cannot name. And in the creation bethink you first, I pray you, of the original cause of all things that are made, the Father; of the creative cause, the Son; of the perfecting cause, the Spirit; so that the ministering spirits subsist by the will of the Father, are brought into being by the operation of the Son, and perfected by the presence of the Spirit. Moreover, the perfection of

angels is sanctification and continuance in it. And let no one imagine me either to affirm that there are three original hypostases or to allege the operation of the Son to be imperfect. For the first principle of existing things is One, creating through the Son and perfecting through the Spirit. The operation of the Father who works all in all is not imperfect, neither is the creating work of the Son incomplete if not perfected by the Spirit. The Father, who creates by His sole will, could not stand in any need of the Son, but nevertheless He wills through the Son; nor could the Son, who works according to the likeness of the Father, need co-operation, but the Son too wills to make perfect through the Spirit. "For by the word of the Lord were the heavens made, and all the host of them by the breath [the Spirit] of His mouth." The Word then is not a mere significant impression on the air, borne by the organs of speech; nor is the Spirit of His mouth a vapor, emitted by the organs of respiration; but the Word is He who "was with God in the beginning" and "was God," John 1:1, and the Spirit of the mouth of God is "the Spirit of truth which proceeds from the Father." John 15:26. You are therefore to perceive three, the Lord who gives the order, the Word who creates, and the Spirit who confirms. And what other thing could confirmation be than the perfecting according to holiness? This perfecting expresses the confirmation's firmness, unchangeableness, and fixity in good. But there is no sanctification without the Spirit. The powers of the heavens are not holy by nature; were it so there would in this respect be no difference between them and the Holy Spirit. It is in proportion to their relative excellence that they have their meed of holiness from the Spirit. The branding-iron is conceived of together with the fire; and yet the material and the fire are distinct. Thus too in the case of the heavenly powers; their substance is, perhaps, an aerial spirit, or an immaterial fire, as it is written, "Who makes his angels spirits and his ministers a flame of fire;" wherefore they exist in space and become visible, and appear in their proper bodily form to them that are worthy. But their sanctification, being external to their substance, super induces their perfection through the communion of the Spirit. They keep their rank by their abiding in the good and true, and while they retain their freedom of will, never fall away from their patient attendance on Him who is truly good. It results that, if by your argument you do away with the Spirit, the hosts of the angels are disbanded, the dominions of archangels are destroyed, all is thrown into confusion, and their life loses law, order, and distinctness. For how are angels to cry "Glory to God in the highest," Luke 2:14, without being empowered by the Spirit? For "No man can say that Jesus is the Lord but by the Holy Ghost, and no man speaking by the Spirit of God calls Jesus accursed;" 1 Corinthians 12:3, as might be said by wicked and hostile spirits, whose fall establishes our statement of the freedom of the will of the invisible powers; being, as they are, in a condition of equipoise between virtue and vice, and on this account needing the succour of the Spirit. I indeed maintain that even Gabriel, Luke 1:11, in no other way foretells events to come than by the foreknowledge of the Spirit, by reason of the fact that one of the boons distributed by the Spirit is prophecy. And whence did he who was ordained to announce the mysteries of the vision to the Man of Desires derive the wisdom whereby he was enabled to teach hidden things, if not from the Holy Spirit? The revelation of mysteries is indeed the peculiar function of the Spirit, as it is written, "God has revealed them unto us by His Spirit." 1 Corinthians 2:10, And how could "thrones, dominions, principalities and powers" Colossians 1:16, live their blessed life, did they not "behold the face of the Father which is in heaven"? Matthew 18:10. But to behold it is impossible without the Spirit! Just as at night, if you withdraw the light from the house, the eyes fall blind and their faculties become inactive, and the worth of objects cannot be discerned, and gold is trodden on in ignorance as though it were iron, so in the order of the intellectual world it is impossible for the high life of Law to abide without the Spirit. For it so to abide were as likely as that an army should maintain its discipline in the absence of its commander, or a chorus its harmony without the guidance of the Coryphæus. How could the Seraphim cry "Holy, Holy, Holy," Isaiah 6:3, were they not taught by the Spirit how often true religion requires them to lift their voice in this ascription of glory? Do "all His angels" and "all His hosts" praise God? It is through the co-operation of the Spirit. Do "thousand thousand" of angels stand before Him, and "ten thousand times ten thousand" ministering spirits? Daniel 7:10. They are blamelessly doing their proper work by the power of the Spirit. All the glorious and unspeakable harmony of the highest heavens both in the service of God, and in the mutual concord of the celestial powers, can therefore only be preserved by the direction of the Spirit. Thus with those beings who are not gradually perfected by increase and advance, but are perfect from the moment of the creation, there is in creation the presence of the Holy Spirit, who confers on them the grace that flows from Him for the completion and perfection of their essence.

    39. But when we speak of the dispensations made for man by our great God and Saviour Jesus Christ, who will gainsay their having been accomplished through the grace of the Spirit? Whether you wish to examine ancient evidence—the blessings of the patriarchs, the succour given through the legislation, the types, the prophecies, the valorous feats in war, the signs wrought through just men;—or on the other hand the things done in the dispensation of the coming of our Lord in the flesh—all is through the Spirit. In the first place He was made an unction, and being inseparably present was with the very flesh of the Lord, according to that which is written, "Upon whom you shall see the

Spirit descending and remaining on Him, the same is," John 1:33, "my beloved Son;" Matthew 3:17, and "Jesus of Nazareth" whom "God anointed with the Holy Ghost." Acts 10:38. After this every operation was wrought with the co-operation of the Spirit. He was present when the Lord was being tempted by the devil; for, it is said, "Jesus was led up of the Spirit into the wilderness to be tempted." Matthew 4:1. He was inseparably with Him while working His wonderful works; for, it is said, "If I by the Spirit of God cast out devils." Matthew 12:28. And He did not leave Him when He had risen from the dead; for when renewing man, and, by breathing on the face of the disciples, restoring the grace, that came of the inbreathing of God, which man had lost, what did the Lord say? "Receive the Holy Ghost: whose soever sins ye remit, they are remitted unto them; and whose soever ye retain, they are retained." John 20:22-23. And is it not plain and incontestable that the ordering of the Church is effected through the Spirit? For He gave, it is said, "in the church, first Apostles, secondarily prophets, thirdly teachers, after that miracles, then gifts of healing, helps, governments, diversities of tongues," 1 Corinthians 12:28, for this order is ordained in accordance with the division of the gifts that are of the Spirit.

40. Moreover by any one who carefully uses his reason it will be found that even at the moment of the expected appearance of the Lord from heaven the Holy Spirit will not, as some suppose, have no functions to discharge: on the contrary, even in the day of His revelation, in which the blessed and only potentate, 1 Timothy 6:15, will judge the world in righteousness, Acts 17:31, the Holy Spirit will be present with Him. For who is so ignorant of the good things prepared by God for them that are worthy, as not to know that the crown of the righteous is the grace of the Spirit, bestowed in more abundant and perfect measure in that day, when spiritual glory shall be distributed to each in proportion as he shall have nobly played the man? For among the glories of the saints are "many mansions" in the Father's house, that is differences of dignities: for as "star differs from star in glory, so also is the resurrection of the dead." 1 Corinthians 15:41-42. They, then, that were sealed by the Spirit unto the day of redemption, and preserve pure and undiminished the first fruits which they received of the Spirit, are they that shall hear the words "well done thou good and faithful servant; you have been faithful over a few things, I will make you ruler over many things." Matthew 25:21. In like manner they which have grieved the Holy Spirit by the wickedness of their ways, or have not wrought for Him that gave to them, shall be deprived of what they have received, their grace being transferred to others; or, according to one of the evangelists, they shall even be wholly cut asunder, Matthew 24:51—the cutting asunder meaning complete separation from the Spirit. The body is not divided, part being delivered to chastisement, and part let off; for when a whole has sinned it were

like the old fables, and unworthy of a righteous judge, for only the half to suffer chastisement. Nor is the soul cut in two—that soul the whole of which possesses the sinful affection throughout, and works the wickedness in co-operation with the body. The cutting asunder, as I have observed, is the separation for aye of the soul from the Spirit. For now, although the Spirit does not suffer admixture with the unworthy, He nevertheless does seem in a manner to be present with them that have once been sealed, awaiting the salvation which follows on their conversion; but then He will be wholly cut off from the soul that has defiled His grace. For this reason "In Hell there is none that makes confession; in death none that remembers God," because the succour of the Spirit is no longer present. How then is it possible to conceive that the judgment is accomplished without the Holy Spirit, wherein the word points out that He is Himself the prize, Philippians 3:14, of the righteous, when instead of the earnest is given that which is perfect, and the first condemnation of sinners, when they are deprived of that which they seem to have? But the greatest proof of the conjunction of the Spirit with the Father and the Son is that He is said to have the same relation to God which the spirit in us has to each of us. "For what man" it is said, "knows the things of a man, save the spirit of man which is in him? Even so the things of God knows no man but the Spirit of God." 1 Corinthians 2:11.

On this point I have said enough.

Chapter 17

Against those who say that the Holy Ghost is not to be numbered with, but numbered under, the Father and the Son. Wherein moreover there is a summary notice of the faith concerning right sub-numeration.

41. What, however, they call sub-numeration, and in what sense they use this word, cannot even be imagined without difficulty. It is well known that it was imported into our language from the "wisdom of the world;" but a point for our present consideration will be whether it has any immediate relation to the subject under discussion. Those who are adepts in vain investigations tell us that, while some nouns are common and of widely extended denotation, others are more specific, and that the force of some is more limited than that of others. Essence, for instance, is a common noun, predicable of all things both animate and inanimate; while animal is more specific, being predicated of fewer subjects than the former, though of more than those which are considered under it, as it embraces both rational and irrational nature. Again, human is more specific than animal, and man than human, and than man the individual Peter, Paul, or John. Do they then mean by sub-numeration the division of the common into its subordinate parts?

But I should hesitate to believe they have reached such a pitch of infatuation as to assert that the God of the universe, like some common quality conceivable only by reason and without actual existence in any hypostasis, is divided into subordinate divisions, and that then this subdivision is called sub-numeration. This would hardly be said even by men melancholy mad, for, besides its impiety, they are establishing the very opposite argument to their own contention. For the subdivisions are of the same essence as that from which they have been divided. The very obviousness of the absurdity makes it difficult for us to find arguments to confute their unreasonableness; so that really their folly looks like an advantage to them; just as soft and yielding bodies offer no resistance, and therefore cannot be struck a stout blow. It is impossible to bring a vigorous confutation to bear on a palpable absurdity. The only course open to us is to pass by their abominable impiety in silence. Yet our love for the brethren and the importunity of our opponents makes silence impossible.

42. What is it that they maintain? Look at the terms of their imposture. "We assert that connumeration is appropriate to subjects of equal dignity, and sub-numeration to those which vary in the direction of inferiority." "Why," I rejoined, do you say this? I fail to understand your extraordinary wisdom. Do you mean that gold is numbered with gold, and that lead is unworthy of the connumeration, but, because of the cheapness of the material, is subnumerated to gold? And do you attribute so much importance to number as that it can either exalt the value of what is cheap, or destroy the dignity of what is valuable? Therefore, again, you will number gold under precious stones, and such precious stones as are smaller and without lustre under those which are larger and brighter in color. But what will not be said by men who spend their time in nothing else but either 'to tell or to hear some new thing'? Acts 17:21. Let these supporters of impiety be classed for the future with Stoics and Epicureans. What sub-numeration is even possible of things less valuable in relation to things very valuable? How is a brass obol to be numbered under a golden stater? "Because," they reply, "we do not speak of possessing two coins, but one and one." But which of these is subnumerated to the other? Each is similarly mentioned. If then you number each by itself, you cause an equality value by numbering them in the same way but, if you join them, you make their value one by numbering them one with the other. But if the sub-numeration belongs to the one which is numbered second, then it is in the power of the counter to begin by counting the brass coin. Let us, however, pass over the confutation of their ignorance, and turn our argument to the main topic.

43. Do you maintain that the Son is numbered under the Father, and the Spirit under the Son, or do you confine your sub-numeration to the Spirit alone? If, on the other hand, you apply this sub-numeration

also to the Son, you revive what is the same impious doctrine, the unlikeness of the substance, the lowliness of rank, the coming into being in later time, and once for all, by this one term, you will plainly again set circling all the blasphemies against the Only-begotten. To controvert these blasphemies would be a longer task than my present purpose admits of; and I am the less bound to undertake it because the impiety has been refuted elsewhere to the best of my ability. If on the other hand they suppose the sub-numeration to benefit the Spirit alone, they must be taught that the Spirit is spoken of together with the Lord in precisely the same manner in which the Son is spoken of with the Father. "The name of the Father and of the Son and of the Holy Ghost," Matthew 28:19, is delivered in like manner, and, according to the co-ordination of words delivered in baptism, the relation of the Spirit to the Son is the same as that of the Son to the Father. And if the Spirit is co-ordinate with the Son, and the Son with the Father, it is obvious that the Spirit is also co-ordinate with the Father. When then the names are ranked in one and the same co-ordinate series, what room is there for speaking on the one hand of connumeration, and on the other of sub-numeration? Nay, without exception, what thing ever lost its own nature by being numbered? Is it not the fact that things when numbered remain what they naturally and originally were, while number is adopted among us as a sign indicative of the plurality of subjects? For some bodies we count, some we measure, and some we weigh; those which are by nature continuous we apprehend by measure; to those which are divided we apply number (with the exception of those which on account of their fineness are measured); while heavy objects are distinguished by the inclination of the balance. It does not however follow that, because we have invented for our convenience symbols to help us to arrive at the knowledge of quantity, we have therefore changed the nature of the things signified. We do not speak of "weighing under" one another things which are weighed, even though one be gold and the other tin; nor yet do we "measure under" things that are measured; and so in the same way we will not "number under" things which are numbered. And if none of the rest of things admits of sub-numeration how can they allege that the Spirit ought to be subnumerated? Labouring as they do under heathen unsoundness, they imagine that things which are inferior, either by grade of rank or subjection of substance, ought to be subnumerated.

Chapter 18

In what manner in the confession of the three hypostases we preserve the pious dogma of the Monarchia. Wherein also is the refutation of them that allege that the Spirit is subnumerated.

44. In delivering the formula of the Father, the Son, and the Holy Ghost, Matthew 28:19, our Lord did not connect the gift with number. He did not say "into First, Second, and Third," nor yet into one, two, and three, but He gave us the boon of the knowledge of the faith which leads to salvation, by means of holy names. So that what saves us is our faith. Number has been devised as a symbol indicative of the quantity of objects. But these men, who bring ruin on themselves from every possible source, have turned even the capacity for counting against the faith. Nothing else undergoes any change in consequence of the addition of number, and yet these men in the case of the divine nature pay reverence to number, lest they should exceed the limits of the honor due to the Paraclete. But, O wisest sirs, let the unapproachable be altogether above and beyond number, as the ancient reverence of the Hebrews wrote the unutterable name of God in peculiar characters, thus endeavouring to set forth its infinite excellence. Count, if you must; but you must not by counting do damage to the faith. Either let the ineffable be honoured by silence; or let holy things be counted consistently with true religion. There is one God and Father, one Only-begotten, and one Holy Ghost. We proclaim each of the hypostases singly; and, when count we must, we do not let an ignorant arithmetic carry us away to the idea of a plurality of Gods.

45. For we do not count by way of addition, gradually making increase from unity to multitude, and saying one, two, and three—nor yet first, second, and third. For "I," God, "am the first, and I am the last." Isaiah 44:6. And hitherto we have never, even at the present time, heard of a second God. Worshipping as we do God of God, we both confess the distinction of the Persons, and at the same time abide by the Monarchy. We do not fritter away the theology in a divided plurality, because one Form, so to say, united in the invariableness of the Godhead, is beheld in God the Father, and in God the Only begotten. For the Son is in the Father and the Father in the Son; since such as is the latter, such is the former, and such as is the former, such is the latter; and herein is the Unity. So that according to the distinction of Persons, both are one and one, and according to the community of Nature, one. How, then, if one and one, are there not two Gods? Because we speak of a king, and of the king's image, and not of two kings. The majesty is not cloven in two, nor the glory divided. The sovereignty and authority over us is one, and so the doxology ascribed

by us is not plural but one; because the honor paid to the image passes on to the prototype. Now what in the one case the image is by reason of imitation, that in the other case the Son is by nature; and as in works of art the likeness is dependent on the form, so in the case of the divine and uncompounded nature the union consists in the communion of the Godhead. One, moreover, is the Holy Spirit, and we speak of Him singly, conjoined as He is to the one Father through the one Son, and through Himself completing the adorable and blessed Trinity. Of Him the intimate relationship to the Father and the Son is sufficiently declared by the fact of His not being ranked in the plurality of the creation, but being spoken of singly; for he is not one of many, but One. For as there is one Father and one Son, so is there one Holy Ghost. He is consequently as far removed from created Nature as reason requires the singular to be removed from compound and plural bodies; and He is in such wise united to the Father and to the Son as unit has affinity with unit.

46. And it is not from this source alone that our proofs of the natural communion are derived, but from the fact that He is moreover said to be "of God;" 2 Corinthians 1:12, not indeed in the sense in which "all things are of God," but in the sense of proceeding out of God, not by generation, like the Son, but as Breath of His mouth. But in no way is the "mouth" a member, nor the Spirit breath that is dissolved; but the word "mouth" is used so far as it can be appropriate to God, and the Spirit is a Substance having life, gifted with supreme power of sanctification. Thus the close relation is made plain, while the mode of the ineffable existence is safeguarded. He is moreover styled 'Spirit of Christ,' as being by nature closely related to Him. Wherefore "If any man have not the Spirit of Christ, he is none of His." Romans 8:9. Hence He alone worthily glorifies the Lord, for, it is said, "He shall glorify me," John 16:14, not as the creature, but as "Spirit of truth," John 14:17, clearly showing forth the truth in Himself, and, as Spirit of wisdom, in His own greatness revealing "Christ the Power of God and the wisdom of God." 1 Corinthians 1:24. And as Paraclete He expresses in Himself the goodness of the Paraclete who sent Him, and in His own dignity manifests the majesty of Him from whom He proceeded. There is then on the one hand a natural glory, as light is the glory of the sun; and on the other a glory bestowed judicially and of free will 'ab extra' on them that are worthy. The latter is twofold. "A son," it is said, "honors his father, and a servant his master." Malachi 1:6. Of these two the one, the servile, is given by the creature; the other, which may be called the intimate, is fulfilled by the Spirit. For, as our Lord said of Himself, "I have glorified You on the earth: I have finished the work which you gave me to do;" John 17:4, so of the Paraclete He says "He shall glorify me: for He shall receive of mine, and shall show it unto you." John 16:14. And as the Son is glorified of the Father when He

says "I have both glorified it and will glorify it again," John 12:28, so is the Spirit glorified through His communion with both Father and Son, and through the testimony of the Only-begotten when He says "All manner of sin and blasphemy shall be forgiven unto men: but the blasphemy against the Holy Ghost shall not be forgiven unto men." Matthew 12:31.

47. And when, by means of the power that enlightens us, we fix our eyes on the beauty of the image of the invisible God, and through the image are led up to the supreme beauty of the spectacle of the archetype, then, I ween, is with us inseparably the Spirit of knowledge, in Himself bestowing on them that love the vision of the truth the power of beholding the Image, not making the exhibition from without, but in Himself leading on to the full knowledge. "No man knows the Father save the Son." And so "no man can say that Jesus is the Lord but by the Holy Ghost." 1 Corinthians 12:3. For it is not said through the Spirit, but by the Spirit, and "God is a spirit, and they that worship Him must worship Him in spirit and in truth," John 4:24, as it is written "in your light shall we see light," namely by the illumination of the Spirit, "the true light which lights every man that comes into the world." John 1:9. It results that in Himself He shows the glory of the Only begotten, and on true worshippers He in Himself bestows the knowledge of God. Thus the way of the knowledge of God lies from One Spirit through the One Son to the One Father, and conversely the natural Goodness and the inherent Holiness and the royal Dignity extend from the Father through the Only-begotten to the Spirit. Thus there is both acknowledgment of the hypostases and the true dogma of the Monarchy is not lost. They on the other hand who support their sub-numeration by talking of first and second and third ought to be informed that into the undefiled theology of Christians they are importing the polytheism of heathen error. No other result can be achieved by the fell device of sub-numeration than the confession of a first, a second, and a third God. For us is sufficient the order prescribed by the Lord. He who confuses this order will be no less guilty of transgressing the law than are the impious heathen.

Enough has been now said to prove, in contravention of their error, that the communion of Nature is in no wise dissolved by the manner of sub-numeration. Let us, however, make a concession to our contentious and feeble minded adversary, and grant that what is second to anything is spoken of in sub-numeration to it. Now let us see what follows. "The first man" it is said "is of the earth earthy, the second man is the Lord from heaven." 1 Corinthians 15:47. Again "that was not first which is spiritual but that which is natural and afterward that which is spiritual." 1 Corinthians 15:46. If then the second is subnumerated to the first, and the subnumerated is inferior in dignity to that to which it was subnumerated, according to you the spiritual is inferior in honor to the natural, and the heavenly man to the earthy.

Chapter 19

Against those who assert that the Spirit ought not to be glorified.

48. "Be it so," it is rejoined, "but glory is by no means so absolutely due to the Spirit as to require His exaltation by us in doxologies." Whence then could we get demonstrations of the dignity of the Spirit, "passing all understanding," Philippians 4:7, if His communion with the Father and the Son were not reckoned by our opponents as good for testimony of His rank? It is, at all events, possible for us to arrive to a certain extent at intelligent apprehension of the sublimity of His nature and of His unapproachable power, by looking at the meaning of His title, and at the magnitude of His operations, and by His good gifts bestowed on us or rather on all creation. He is called Spirit, as "God is a Spirit," John 4:24, and "the breath of our nostrils, the anointed of the Lord." He is called holy, 1 John 1:20, as the Father is holy, and the Son is holy, for to the creature holiness was brought in from without, but to the Spirit holiness is the fulfillment of nature, and it is for this reason that He is described not as being sanctified, but as sanctifying. He is called good, as the Father is good, and He who was begotten of the Good is good, and to the Spirit His goodness is essence. He is called upright, as "the Lord is upright," in that He is Himself truth, and is Himself Righteousness, 2 Corinthians 3:8-9, having no divergence nor leaning to one side or to the other, on account of the immutability of His substance. He is called Paraclete, like the Only begotten, as He Himself says, "I will ask the Father, and He will give you another comforter." Thus names are borne by the Spirit in common with the Father and the Son, and He gets these titles from His natural and close relationship. From what other source could they be derived? Again He is called royal, Spirit of truth, and Spirit of wisdom. Isaiah 11:2. "The Spirit of God," it is said "has made me," Job 33:4, and God filled Bezaleel with "the divine Spirit of wisdom and understanding and knowledge." Such names as these are super-eminent and mighty, but they do not transcend His glory.

49. And His operations, what are they? For majesty ineffable, and for numbers innumerable. How shall we form a conception of what extends beyond the ages? What were His operations before that creation whereof we can conceive? How great the grace which He conferred on creation? What the power exercised by Him over the ages to come? He existed; He pre-existed; He co-existed with the Father and the Son before the ages. It follows that, even if you can conceive of anything beyond the ages, you will find the Spirit yet further above and beyond. And if you think of the creation, the powers of the heavens

were established by the Spirit, the establishment being understood to refer to disability to fall away from good. For it is from the Spirit that the powers derive their close relationship to God, their inability to change to evil, and their continuance in blessedness. Is it Christ's advent? The Spirit is forerunner. Is there the incarnate presence? The Spirit is inseparable. Working of miracles, and gifts of healing are through the Holy Spirit. Demons were driven out by the Spirit of God. The devil was brought to naught by the presence of the Spirit. Remission of sins was by the gift of the Spirit, for "you were washed, you were sanctified,... in the name of the Lord Jesus Christ, and in the holy Spirit of our God." There is close relationship with God through the Spirit, for "God has sent forth the Spirit of His Son into your hearts, crying Abba, Father." Galatians 4:6. The resurrection from the dead is effected by the operation of the Spirit, for "You send forth your spirit, they are created; and You renew the face of the earth." If here creation may be taken to mean the bringing of the departed to life again, how mighty is not the operation of the Spirit, Who is to us the dispenser of the life that follows on the resurrection, and attunes our souls to the spiritual life beyond? Or if here by creation is meant the change to a better condition of those who in this life have fallen into sin, (for it is so understood according to the usage of Scripture, as in the words of Paul "if any man be in Christ he is a new creature"), 2 Corinthians 5:17, the renewal which takes place in this life, and the transmutation from our earthly and sensuous life to the heavenly conversation which takes place in us through the Spirit, then our souls are exalted to the highest pitch of admiration. With these thoughts before us are we to be afraid of going beyond due bounds in the extravagance of the honor we pay? Shall we not rather fear lest, even though we seem to give Him the highest names which the thoughts of man can conceive or man's tongue utter, we let our thoughts about Him fall too low?

It is the Spirit which says, as the Lord says, "Get you down, and go with them, doubting nothing: for I have sent them." Acts 10:20. Are these the words of an inferior, or of one in dread? "Separate me Barnabas and Saul for the work whereunto I have called them." Acts 13:2. Does a slave speak thus? And Isaiah, "The Lord God and His Spirit has sent me," and "the Spirit came down from the Lord and guided them." And pray do not again understand by this guidance some humble service, for the Word witnesses that it was the work of God— "You led your people," it is said "like a flock," and "You that leads Joseph like a flock," and "He led them on safely, so that they feared not." Thus when you hear that when the Comforter has come, He will put you in remembrance, and "guide you into all truth," do not misrepresent the meaning.

50. But, it is said that "He makes intercession for us." Romans 8:26-27. It follows then that, as the suppliant is inferior to the

benefactor, so far is the Spirit inferior in dignity to God. But have you never heard concerning the Only-begotten that He "is at the right hand of God, who also makes intercession for us"? Romans 8:34. Do not, then, because the Spirit is in you—if indeed He is at all in you—nor yet because He teaches us who were blinded, and guides us to the choice of what profits us—do not for this reason allow yourself to be deprived of the right and holy opinion concerning Him. For to make the loving kindness of your benefactor a ground of ingratitude were indeed a very extravagance of unfairness. "Grieve not the Holy Spirit;" Ephesians 4:30, hear the words of Stephen, the first fruits of the martyrs, when he reproaches the people for their rebellion and disobedience; "you do always," he says, "resist the Holy Ghost;" Acts 7:51, and again Isaiah,—"They vexed His Holy Spirit, therefore He was turned to be their enemy;" Isaiah 63:10, and in another passage, "the house of Jacob angered the Spirit of the Lord." Are not these passages indicative of authoritative power? I leave it to the judgment of my readers to determine what opinions we ought to hold when we hear these passages; whether we are to regard the Spirit as an instrument, a subject, of equal rank with the creature, and a fellow servant of ourselves, or whether, on the contrary, to the ears of the pious the mere whisper of this blasphemy is not most grievous. Do you call the Spirit a servant? But, it is said, "the servant knows not what his Lord does," John 15:15 and yet the Spirit knows the things of God, as "the spirit of man that is in him." 1 Corinthians 2:11.

Chapter 20

Against those who maintain that the Spirit is in the rank neither of a servant nor of a master, but in that of the free.

51. He is not a slave, it is said; not a master, but free. Oh the terrible insensibility, the pitiable audacity, of them that maintain this! Shall I rather lament in them their ignorance or their blasphemy? They try to insult the doctrines that concern the divine nature by comparing them with the human, and endeavour to apply to the ineffable nature of God that common custom of human life whereby the difference of degrees is variable, not perceiving that among men no one is a slave by nature. For men are either brought under a yoke of slavery by conquest, as when prisoners are taken in war; or they are enslaved on account of poverty, as the Egyptians were oppressed by Pharaoh; or, by a wise and mysterious dispensation, the worst children are by their fathers' order condemned to serve the wiser and the better; and this any righteous enquirer into the circumstances would declare to be not a sentence of condemnation but a benefit. For it is more profitable that the man who, through lack of intelligence, has no natural principle of rule within

himself, should become the chattel of another, to the end that, being guided by the reason of his master, he may be like a chariot with a charioteer, or a boat with a steersman seated at the tiller. For this reason Jacob by his father's blessing became lord of Esau, Genesis 27:29, in order that the foolish son, who had not intelligence, his proper guardian, might, even though he wished it not, be benefited by his prudent brother. So Canaan shall be "a servant unto his brethren," Genesis 9:25, because, since his father Ham was unwise, he was uninstructed in virtue. In this world, then, it is thus that men are made slaves, but they who have escaped poverty or war, or do not require the tutelage of others, are free. It follows that even though one man be called master and another servant, nevertheless, both in view of our mutual equality of rank and as chattels of our Creator, we are all fellow slaves. But in that other world what can you bring out of bondage? For no sooner were they created than bondage was commenced. The heavenly bodies exercise no rule over one another, for they are unmoved by ambition, but all bow down to God, and render to Him alike the awe which is due to Him as Master and the glory which falls to Him as Creator. For "a son honors his father and a servant his master," Malachi 1:6, and from all God asks one of these two things; for "if I then be a Father where is my honor? And if I be a Master where is my fear?" Malachi 1:6. Otherwise the life of all men, if it were not under the oversight of a master, would be most pitiable; as is the condition of the apostate powers who, because they stiffen their neck against God Almighty, fling off the reins of their bondage,—not that their natural constitution is different; but the cause is in their disobedient disposition to their Creator. Whom then do you call free? Him who has no King? Him who has neither power to rule another nor willingness to be ruled? Among all existent beings no such nature is to be found. To entertain such a conception of the Spirit is obvious blasphemy. If He is a creature of course He serves with all the rest, for "all things," it is said "are your servants," but if He is above Creation, then He shares in royalty.

Chapter 21

Proof from Scripture that the Spirit is called Lord.

52. But why get an unfair victory for our argument by fighting over these undignified questions, when it is within our power to prove that the excellence of the glory is beyond dispute by adducing more lofty considerations? If, indeed, we repeat what we have been taught by Scripture, every one of the Pneumatomachi will perhaps raise a loud and vehement outcry, stop their ears, pick up stones or anything else that comes to hand for a weapon, and charge against us. But our own

Saint Basil

security must not be regarded by us before the truth. We have learned from the Apostle, "the Lord direct your hearts into the love of God and into the patient waiting for Christ" for our tribulations. Who is the Lord that directs into the love of God and into the patient waiting for Christ for tribulations? Let those men answer us who are for making a slave of the Holy Spirit. For if the argument had been about God the Father, it would certainly have said, 'the Lord direct you into His own love,' or if about the Son, it would have added 'into His own patience.' Let them then seek what other Person there is who is worthy to be honoured with the title of Lord. And parallel with this is that other passage, "and the Lord make you to increase and abound in love one toward another, and toward all men, even as we do towards you; to the end He may establish your hearts unblamable in holiness before God, even our Father, at the coming of our Lord Jesus Christ with all His saints." 1 Thessalonians 3:12-13. Now what Lord does he entreat to establish the hearts of the faithful at Thessalonica, unblamable in holiness before God even our Father, at the coming of our Lord? Let those answer who place the Holy Ghost among the ministering spirits that are sent forth on service. They cannot. Wherefore let them hear yet another testimony which distinctly calls the Spirit Lord. "The Lord," it is said, "is that Spirit;" and again "even as from the Lord the Spirit." But to leave no ground for objection, I will quote the actual words of the Apostle;— "For even unto this day remains the same veil untaken away in the reading of the Old Testament, which veil is done away in Christ.... Nevertheless, when it shall turn to the Lord, the veil shall be taken away. Now the Lord is that Spirit." Why does he speak thus? Because he who abides in the bare sense of the letter, and in it busies himself with the observances of the Law, has, as it were, got his own heart enveloped in the Jewish acceptance of the letter, like a veil; and this befalls him because of his ignorance that the bodily observance of the Law is done away by the presence of Christ, in that for the future the types are transferred to the reality. Lamps are made needless by the advent of the sun; and, on the appearance of the truth, the occupation of the Law is gone, and prophecy is hushed into silence. He, on the contrary, who has been empowered to look down into the depth of the meaning of the Law, and, after passing through the obscurity of the letter, as through a veil, to arrive within things unspeakable, is like Moses taking off the veil when he spoke with God. He, too, turns from the letter to the Spirit. So with the veil on the face of Moses corresponds the obscurity of the teaching of the Law, and spiritual contemplation with the turning to the Lord. He, then, who in the reading of the Law takes away the letter and turns to the Lord,—and the Lord is now called the Spirit—becomes moreover like Moses, who had his face glorified by the manifestation of God. For just as objects which lie near brilliant colors are themselves tinted by the brightness which is shed around, so is he who fixes his gaze firmly on the Spirit by the Spirit's glory somehow transfigured into greater splendour, having his heart lighted up, as it were, by some light streaming from the truth of the Spirit. And, this is "being changed from the glory" of the Spirit "into" His own "glory," not in niggard degree, nor dimly and indistinctly, but as we might expect any one to be who is enlightened by the Spirit. Do you not, O man, fear the Apostle when he says "You are the temple of God, and the Spirit of God dwells in you"? 1 Corinthians 3:16. Could he ever have brooked to honor with the title of "temple" the quarters of a slave? How can he who calls Scripture "God-inspired," 2 Timothy 3:16, because it was written through the inspiration of the Spirit, use the language of one who insults and belittles Him?

Chapter 22

Establishment of the natural communion of the Spirit from His being, equally with the Father and the Son, unapproachable in thought.

53. Moreover the surpassing excellence of the nature of the Spirit is to be learned not only from His having the same title as the Father and the Son, and sharing in their operations, but also from His being, like the Father and the Son, unapproachable in thought. For what our Lord says of the Father as being above and beyond human conception, and what He says of the Son, this same language He uses also of the Holy Ghost. "O righteous Father," He says, "the world has not known You," John 17:25, meaning here by the world not the complex whole compounded of heaven and earth, but this life of ours subject to death, and exposed to innumerable vicissitudes. And when discoursing of Himself He says, "Yet a little while and the world sees me no more, but you see me;" John 14:19, again in this passage, applying the word world to those who being bound down by this material and carnal life, and beholding the truth by material sight alone, were ordained, through their unbelief in the resurrection, to see our Lord no more with the eyes of the heart. And He said the same concerning the Spirit. "The Spirit of truth," He says, "whom the world cannot receive, because it sees Him not, neither knows Him: but you know Him, for He dwells with you." John 14:17. For the carnal man, who has never trained his mind to contemplation, but rather keeps it buried deep in lust of the flesh, as in mud, is powerless to look up to the spiritual light of the truth. And so the world, that is life enslaved by the affections of the flesh, can no more receive the grace of the Spirit than a weak eye the light of a sunbeam. But the Lord, who by His teaching bore witness to purity of life, gives to His disciples the power of now both beholding and contemplating the Spirit. For "now," He says, "You are clean through

the word which I have spoken unto you," John 15:3, wherefore "the world cannot receive Him, because it sees Him not,... but you know Him; for he dwells with you." John 14:17 And so says Isaiah;—"He that spread forth the earth and that which comes out of it; he that gives breath unto the people upon it, and Spirit to them that trample on it"; for they that trample down earthly things and rise above them are borne witness to as worthy of the gift of the Holy Ghost. What then ought to be thought of Him whom the world cannot receive, and Whom saints alone can contemplate through pureness of heart? What kind of honors can be deemed adequate to Him?

Chapter 23

The glorifying of the enumeration of His attributes.

54. Now of the rest of the Powers each is believed to be in a circumscribed place. The angel who stood by Cornelius, Acts 10:3, was not at one and the same moment with Philip; Acts 8:26, nor yet did the angel who spoke with Zacharias from the altar at the same time occupy his own post in heaven. But the Spirit is believed to have been operating at the same time in Habakkuk and in Daniel at Babylon, and to have been at the prison with Jeremiah, and with Ezekiel at the Chebar. Ezekiel 1:1. For the Spirit of the Lord fills the world, Wisdom 1:7, and "whither shall I go from your spirit? Or whither shall I flee from your presence?" And, in the words of the Prophet, "For I am with you, says the Lord... and my spirit remains among you." Haggai 2:4-5. But what nature is it becoming to assign to Him who is omnipresent, and exists together with God? The nature which is all-embracing, or one which is confined to particular places, like that which our argument shows the nature of angels to be? No one would so say. Shall we not then highly exalt Him who is in His nature divine, in His greatness infinite, in His operations powerful, in the blessings He confers, good? Shall we not give Him glory? And I understand glory to mean nothing else than the enumeration of the wonders which are His own. It follows then that either we are forbidden by our antagonists even to mention the good things which flow to us from Him. or on the other hand that the mere recapitulation of His attributes is the fullest possible attribution of glory. For not even in the case of the God and Father of our Lord Jesus Christ and of the Only begotten Son, are we capable of giving Them glory otherwise than by recounting, to the extent of our powers, all the wonders that belong to Them.

Chapter 24

Proof of the absurdity of the refusal to glorify the Spirit, from the comparison of things glorified in creation.

55. Furthermore man is "crowned with glory and honor," and "glory, honor and peace" are laid up by promise "to every man that works good." Romans 2:10. There is moreover a special and peculiar glory for Israelites "to whom," it is said "pertains the adoption and the glory... and the service," Romans 9:4, and the Psalmist speaks of a certain glory of his own, "that my glory may sing praise to You;" and again "Awake up my glory" and according to the Apostle there is a certain glory of sun and moon and stars, and "the ministration of condemnation is glorious." 2 Corinthians 3:9. While then so many things are glorified, do you wish the Spirit alone of all things to be unglorified? Yet the Apostle says "the ministration of the Spirit is glorious." 2 Corinthians 3:8. How then can He Himself be unworthy of glory? How according to the Psalmist can the glory of the just man be great and according to you the glory of the Spirit none? How is there not a plain peril from such arguments of our bringing on ourselves the sin from which there is no escape? If the man who is being saved by works of righteousness glorifies even them that fear the Lord much less would he deprive the Spirit of the glory which is His due.

Grant, they say, that He is to be glorified, but not with the Father and the Son. But what reason is there in giving up the place appointed by the Lord for the Spirit, and inventing some other? What reason is there for robbing of His share of glory Him Who is everywhere associated with the Godhead; in the confession of the Faith, in the baptism of redemption, in the working of miracles, in the indwelling of the saints, in the graces bestowed on obedience? For there is not even one single gift which reaches creation without the Holy Ghost; when not even a single word can be spoken in defense of Christ except by them that are aided by the Spirit, as we have learned in the Gospels from our Lord and Saviour. Matthew 10:19-20. And I know not whether any one who has been partaker of the Holy Spirit will consent that we should overlook all this, forget His fellowship in all things, and tear the Spirit asunder from the Father and the Son. Where then are we to take Him and rank Him? With the creature? Yet all the creature is in bondage, but the Spirit makes free. "And where the Spirit of the Lord is, there is liberty." 2 Corinthians 3:17. Many arguments might be adduced to them that it is unseemly to coordinate the Holy Spirit with created nature, but for the present I will pass them by. Were I indeed to bring forward, in a manner befitting the dignity of the discussion, all the proofs always available on our side, and so overthrow the

Saint Basil 55

objections of our opponents, a lengthy dissertation would be required, and my readers might be worn out by my prolixity. I therefore propose to reserve this matter for a special treatise, and to apply myself to the points now more immediately before us.

56. Let us then examine the points one by one. He is good by nature, in the same way as the Father is good, and the Son is good; the creature on the other hand shares in goodness by choosing the good. He knows "The deep things of God;" 1 Corinthians 2:10-11, the creature receives the manifestation of ineffable things through the Spirit. He quickens together with God, who produces and preserves all things alive, and together with the Son, who gives life. "He that raised up Christ from the dead," it is said, "shall also quicken your mortal bodies by the spirit that dwells in you;" Romans 8:11, and again "my sheep hear my voice,... and I give unto them eternal life;" John 10:27-28, but "the Spirit" also, it is said, "gives life," 2 Corinthians 3:6 and again "the Spirit," it is said, "is life, because of righteousness." Romans 8:10. And the Lord bears witness that "it is the Spirit that quickens; the flesh profits nothing." John 6:63. How then shall we alienate the Spirit from His quickening power, and make Him belong to lifeless nature? Who is so contentious, who is so utterly without the heavenly gift, and unfed by God's good words, who is so devoid of part and lot in eternal hopes, as to sever the Spirit from the Godhead and rank Him with the creature?

57. Now it is urged that the Spirit is in us as a gift from God, and that the gift is not reverenced with the same honor as that which is attributed to the giver. The Spirit is a gift of God, but a gift of life, for the law of "the Spirit of life," it is said, "has made" us "free;" Romans 8:2, and a gift of power, for "you shall receive power after that the Holy Ghost has come upon you." Acts 1:8. Is He on this account to be lightly esteemed? Did not God also bestow His Son as a free gift to mankind? "He that spared not His own Son," it is said, "but delivered Him up for us all, how shall He not with Him also freely give us all things?" Romans 8:32. And in another place, "that we might truly know the things that are freely given us of God," 1 Corinthians 2:12, in reference to the mystery of the Incarnation. It follows then that the maintainers of such arguments, in making the greatness of God's loving kindness an occasion of blasphemy, have really surpassed the ingratitude of the Jews. They find fault with the Spirit because He gives us freedom to call God our Father. "For God has sent forth the Spirit of His Son into" our "hearts crying Abba, Father," Galatians 4:6, that the voice of the Spirit may become the very voice of them that have received him.

Chapter 25

That Scripture uses the words "in" or "by," ἐν, in place of "with." Wherein also it is proved that the word "and" has the same force as "with."

58. It is, however, asked by our opponents, how it is that Scripture nowhere describes the Spirit as glorified together with the Father and the Son, but carefully avoids the use of the expression "with the Spirit," while it everywhere prefers to ascribe glory "in Him" as being the fitter phrase. I should, for my own part, deny that the word in [or by] implies lower dignity than the word "with;" I should maintain on the contrary that, rightly understood, it leads us up to the highest possible meaning. This is the case where, as we have observed, it often stands instead of with; as for instance, "I will go into your house in burnt offerings," instead of with burnt offerings and "he brought them forth also by silver and gold," that is to say with silver and gold and "you go not forth in our armies" instead of with our armies, and innumerable similar passages. In short I should very much like to learn from this newfangled philosophy what kind of glory the Apostle ascribed by the word in, according to the interpretation which our opponents proffer as derived from Scripture, for I have nowhere found the formula "To You, O Father, be honor and glory, through Your only begotten Son, by [or in] the Holy Ghost,"—a form which to our opponents comes, so to say, as naturally as the air they breathe. You may indeed find each of these clauses separately, but they will nowhere be able to show them to us arranged in this conjunction. If, then, they want exact conformity to what is written, let them give us exact references. If, on the other hand, they make concession to custom, they must not make us an exception to such a privilege.

59. As we find both expressions in use among the faithful, we use both; in the belief that full glory is equally given to the Spirit by both. The mouths, however, of revilers of the truth may best be stopped by the preposition which, while it has the same meaning as that of the Scriptures, is not so wieldy a weapon for our opponents, (indeed it is now an object of their attack) and is used instead of the conjunction and. For to say "Paul and Silvanus and Timothy" 1 Thessalonians 1:1, is precisely the same thing as to say Paul with Timothy and Silvanus; for the connection of the names is preserved by either mode of expression. The Lord says "The Father, the Son and the Holy Ghost." Matthew 28:19. If I say the Father and the Son with the Holy Ghost shall I make, any difference in the sense? Of the connection of names by means of the conjunction and the instances are many. We read "The grace of our Lord Jesus Christ and the love of God and the fellowship

Saint Basil

of the Holy Ghost," 2 Corinthians 13:13, and again "I beseech you for the Lord Jesus Christ's sake, and for the love of the Spirit." Romans 15:30. Now if we wish to use with instead of and, what difference shall we have made? I do not see; unless any one according to hard and fast grammatical rules might prefer the conjunction as copulative and making the union stronger, and reject the preposition as of inferior force. But if we had to defend ourselves on these points I do not suppose we should require a defense of many words. As it is, their argument is not about syllables nor yet about this or that sound of a word, but about things differing most widely in power and in truth. It is for this reason that, while the use of the syllables is really a matter of no importance whatever, our opponents are making the endeavour to authorize some syllables, and hunt out others from the Church. For my own part, although the usefulness of the word is obvious as soon as it is heard, I will nevertheless set forth the arguments which led our fathers to adopt the reasonable course of employing the preposition "with." It does indeed equally well with the preposition "and," confute the mischief of Sabellius; and it sets forth quite as well as "and" the distinction of the hypostases, as in the words "I and my Father will come," and "I and my Father are one." John 10:30. In addition to this the proof it contains of the eternal fellowship and uninterrupted conjunction is excellent. For to say that the Son is with the Father is to exhibit at once the distinction of the hypostases, and the inseparability of the fellowship. The same thing is observable even in mere human matters, for the conjunction "and" intimates that there is a common element in an action, while the preposition "with" declares in some sense as well the communion in action. As, for instance—Paul and Timothy sailed to Macedonia, but both Tychicus and Onesimus were sent to the Colossians. Hence we learn that they did the same thing. But suppose we are told that they sailed with, and were sent with? Then we are informed in addition that they carried out the action in company with one another. Thus while the word "with" upsets the error of Sabellius as no other word can, it routs also sinners who err in the very opposite direction; those, I mean, who separate the Son from the Father and the Spirit from the Son, by intervals of time.

60. As compared with "in," there is this difference, that while "with" sets forth the mutual conjunction of the parties associated—as, for example, of those who sail with, or dwell with, or do anything else in common, "in" shows their relation to that matter in which they happen to be acting. For we no sooner hear the words "sail in" or "dwell in" than we form the idea of the boat or the house. Such is the distinction between these words in ordinary usage; and laborious investigation might discover further illustrations. I have no time to examine into the nature of the syllables. Since then it has been shown that "with" most clearly gives the sense of conjunction, let it be

declared, if you will, to be under safe-conduct, and cease to wage your savage and truceless war against it. Nevertheless, though the word is naturally thus auspicious, yet if any one likes, in the ascription of praise, to couple the names by the syllable "and," and to give glory, as we have taught in the Gospel, in the formula of baptism, Father and Son and Holy Ghost, Matthew 28:19, be it so: no one will make any objection. On these conditions, if you will, let us come to terms. But our foes would rather surrender their tongues than accept this word. It is this that rouses against us their implacable and truceless war. We must offer the ascription of glory to God, it is contended, in the Holy Ghost, and not and to the Holy Ghost, and they passionately cling to this word in, as though it lowered the Spirit. It will therefore be not unprofitable to speak at greater length about it; and I shall be astonished if they do not, when they have heard what we have to urge, reject the in as itself a traitor to their cause, and a deserter to the side of the glory of the Spirit.

Chapter 26

That the word "in," in as many senses as it bears, is understood of the Spirit.

61. Now, short and simple as this utterance is, it appears to me, as I consider it, that its meanings are many and various. For of the senses in which "in" is used, we find that all help our conceptions of the Spirit. Form is said to be in Matter; Power to be in what is capable of it; Habit to be in him who is affected by it; and so on. Therefore, inasmuch as the Holy Spirit perfects rational beings, completing their excellence, He is analogous to Form. For he, who no longer "lives after the flesh," Romans 8:12, but, being "led by the Spirit of God," Romans 8:14, is called a Son of God, being "conformed to the image of the Son of God," Romans 8:29, is described as spiritual. And as is the power of seeing in the healthy eye, so is the operation of the Spirit in the purified soul. Wherefore also Paul prays for the Ephesians that they may have their "eyes enlightened" by "the Spirit of wisdom." Ephesians 1:17-18. And as the art in him who has acquired it, so is the grace of the Spirit in the recipient ever present, though not continuously in operation. For as the art is potentially in the artist, but only in operation when he is working in accordance with it, so also the Spirit is ever present with those that are worthy, but works, as need requires, in prophecies, or in healings, or in some other actual carrying into effect of His potential action. Furthermore as in our bodies is health, or heat, or, generally, their variable conditions, so, very frequently is the Spirit in the soul; since He does not abide with those who, on account of the instability of their will, easily reject the grace which they have received. An instance

of this is seen in Saul, 1 Samuel 16:14, and the seventy elders of the children of Israel, except Eldad and Medad, with whom alone the Spirit appears to have remained, and, generally, any one similar to these in character. And like reason in the soul, which is at one time the thought in the heart, and at another speech uttered by the tongue, so is the Holy Spirit, as when He "bears witness with our spirit," Romans 8:16, and when He "cries in our hearts, Abba, Father," Galatians 6:4, or when He speaks on our behalf, as it is said, "It is not ye that speak, but the Spirit of our Father which speaks in you." Matthew 10:20. Again, the Spirit is conceived of, in relation to the distribution of gifts, as a whole in parts. For we all are "members one of another, having gifts differing according to the grace that is given us." Romans 12:5-6. Wherefore "the eye cannot say to the hand, I have no need of you; nor again the head to the feet, I have no need of you," 1 Corinthians 12:21, but all together complete the Body of Christ in the Unity of the Spirit, and render to one another the needful aid that comes of the gifts. "But God has set the members in the body, every one of them, as it has pleased Him." But "the members have the same care for one another," 1 Corinthians 12:25, according to the inborn spiritual communion of their sympathy. Wherefore, "whether one member suffer, all the members suffer with it; or one member be honoured, all the members rejoice with it." 1 Corinthians 12:26. And as parts in the whole so are we individually in the Spirit, because we all "were baptized in one body into one spirit."

62. It is an extraordinary statement, but it is none the less true, that the Spirit is frequently spoken of as the place of them that are being sanctified, and it will become evident that even by this figure the Spirit, so far from being degraded, is rather glorified. For words applicable to the body are, for the sake of clearness, frequently transferred in scripture to spiritual conceptions. Accordingly we find the Psalmist, even in reference to God, saying "Be Thou to me a champion God and a strong place to save me" and concerning the Spirit "behold there is place by me, and stand upon a rock." Plainly meaning the place or contemplation in the Spirit wherein, after Moses had entered there, he was able to see God intelligibly manifested to him. This is the special and peculiar place of true worship; for it is said "Take heed to yourself that thou offer not your burnt offerings in every place... but in the place the Lord your God shall choose." Deuteronomy 12:13-14. Now what is a spiritual burnt offering? "The sacrifice of praise." And in what place do we offer it? In the Holy Spirit. Where have we learned this? From the Lord himself in the words "The true worshippers shall worship the Father in spirit and in truth." This place Jacob saw and said "The Lord is in this place." Genesis 28:16. It follows that the Spirit is verily the place of the saints and the saint is the proper place for the Spirit, offering himself as he does for the indwelling of God, and called God's

Temple. 1 Corinthians 6:19. So Paul speaks in Christ, saying "In the sight of God we speak in Christ," 2 Corinthians 2:17, and Christ in Paul, as he himself says "Since ye seek a proof of Christ speaking in me." 2 Corinthians 13:3. So also in the Spirit he speaks mysteries, 1 Corinthians 14:2, and again the Spirit speaks in him. 1 Peter 1:11.

63. In relation to the originate, then, the Spirit is said to be in them "in various portions and in various manners," Hebrews 1:1 while in relation to the Father and the Son it is more consistent with true religion to assert Him not to be in but to be with. For the grace flowing from Him when He dwells in those that are worthy, and carries out His own operations, is well described as existing in those that are able to receive Him. On the other hand His essential existence before the ages, and His ceaseless abiding with Son and Father, cannot be contemplated without requiring titles expressive of eternal conjunction. For absolute and real co-existence is predicated in the case of things which are mutually inseparable. We say, for instance, that heat exists in the hot iron, but in the case of the actual fire it co-exists; and, similarly, that health exists in the body, but that life co-exists with the soul. It follows that wherever the fellowship is intimate, congenial, and inseparable, the word with is more expressive, suggesting, as it does, the idea of inseparable fellowship. Where on the other hand the grace flowing from the Spirit naturally comes and goes, it is properly and truly said to exist in, even if on account of the firmness of the recipients' disposition to good the grace abides with them continually. Thus whenever we have in mind the Spirit's proper rank, we contemplate Him as being with the Father and the Son, but when we think of the grace that flows from Him operating on those who participate in it, we say that the Spirit is in us. And the doxology which we offer "in the Spirit" is not an acknowledgment of His rank; it is rather a confession of our own weakness, while we show that we are not sufficient to glorify Him of ourselves, but our sufficiency is in the Holy Spirit. Enabled in, [or by,] Him we render thanks to our God for the benefits we have received, according to the measure of our purification from evil, as we receive one a larger and another a smaller share of the aid of the Spirit, that we may offer "the sacrifice of praise to God." Hebrews 13:15. According to one use, then, it is thus that we offer our thanksgiving, as the true religion requires, in the Spirit; although it is not quite unobjectionable that any one should testify of himself "the Spirit of God is in me, and I offer glory after being made wise through the grace that flows from Him." For to a Paul it is becoming to say "I think also that I have the Spirit of God," 1 Corinthians 7:40, and again, "that good thing which was committed to you keep by the Holy Ghost which dwells in us." 2 Timothy 1:14. And of Daniel it is fitting to say that "the Holy Spirit of God is in him," and similarly of men who are like these in virtue.

64. Another sense may however be given to the phrase, that just as

the Father is seen in the Son, so is the Son in the Spirit. The "worship in the Spirit" suggests the idea of the operation of our intelligence being carried on in the light, as may be learned from the words spoken to the woman of Samaria. Deceived as she was by the customs of her country into the belief that worship was local, our Lord, with the object of giving her better instruction, said that worship ought to be offered "in Spirit and in Truth," John 4:24, plainly meaning by the Truth, Himself. As then we speak of the worship offered in the Image of God the Father as worship in the Son, so too do we speak of worship in the Spirit as showing in Himself the Godhead of the Lord. Wherefore even in our worship the Holy Spirit is inseparable from the Father and the Son. If you remain outside the Spirit you will not be able even to worship at all; and on your becoming in Him you will in no way be able to dissever Him from God—any more than you will divorce light from visible objects. For it is impossible to behold the Image of the invisible God except by the enlightenment of the Spirit, and impracticable for him to fix his gaze on the Image to dissever the light from the Image, because the cause of vision is of necessity seen at the same time as the visible objects. Thus fitly and consistently do we behold the "Brightness of the glory" of God by means of the illumination of the Spirit, and by means of the "Express Image" we are led up to Him of whom He is the Express Image and Seal, graven to the like.

Chapter 27

Of the origin of the word "with," and what force it has. Also concerning the unwritten laws of the church.

65. The word "in," say our opponents, is exactly appropriate to the Spirit, and sufficient for every thought concerning Him. Why then, they ask, have we introduced this new phrase, saying, "with the Spirit" instead of "in the Holy Spirit," thus employing an expression which is quite unnecessary, and sanctioned by no usage in the churches? Now it has been asserted in the previous portion of this treatise that the word "in" has not been specially allotted to the Holy Spirit, but is common to the Father and the Son. It has also been, in my opinion, sufficiently demonstrated that, so far from detracting anything from the dignity of the Spirit, it leads all, but those whose thoughts are wholly perverted, to the sublimest height. It remains for me to trace the origin of the word "with;" to explain what force it has, and to show that it is in harmony with Scripture.

66. Of the beliefs and practices whether generally accepted or publicly enjoined which are preserved in the Church some we possess derived from written teaching; others we have received delivered to us

"in a mystery" by the tradition of the apostles; and both of these in relation to true religion have the same force. And these no one will gainsay—no one, at all events, who is even moderately versed in the institutions of the Church. For were we to attempt to reject such customs as have no written authority, on the ground that the importance they possess is small, we should unintentionally injure the Gospel in its very vitals; or, rather, should make our public definition a mere phrase and nothing more. For instance, to take the first and most general example, who is thence who has taught us in writing to sign with the sign of the cross those who have trusted in the name of our Lord Jesus Christ? What writing has taught us to turn to the East at the prayer? Which of the saints has left us in writing the words of the invocation at the displaying of the bread of the Eucharist and the cup of blessing? For we are not, as is well known, content with what the apostle or the Gospel has recorded, but both in preface and conclusion we add other words as being of great importance to the validity of the ministry, and these we derive from unwritten teaching. Moreover we bless the water of baptism and the oil of the chrism, and besides this the catechumen who is being baptized. On what written authority do we do this? Is not our authority silent and mystical tradition? Nay, by what written word is the anointing of oil itself taught? And whence comes the custom of baptizing thrice? And as to the other customs of baptism from what Scripture do we derive the renunciation of Satan and his angels? Does not this come from that unpublished and secret teaching which our fathers guarded in a silence out of the reach of curious meddling and inquisitive investigation? Well had they learned the lesson that the awful dignity of the mysteries is best preserved by silence. What the uninitiated are not even allowed to look at was hardly likely to be publicly paraded about in written documents. What was the meaning of the mighty Moses in not making all the parts of the tabernacle open to every one? The profane he stationed without the sacred barriers; the first courts he conceded to the purer; the Levites alone he judged worthy of being servants of the Deity; sacrifices and burnt offerings and the rest of the priestly functions he allotted to the priests; one chosen out of all he admitted to the shrine, and even this one not always but on only one day in the year, and of this one day a time was fixed for his entry so that he might gaze on the Holy of Holies amazed at the strangeness and novelty of the sight. Moses was wise enough to know that contempt stretches to the trite and to the obvious, while a keen interest is naturally associated with the unusual and the unfamiliar. In the same manner the Apostles and Fathers who laid down laws for the Church from the beginning thus guarded the awful dignity of the mysteries in secrecy and silence, for what is bruited abroad random among the common folk is no mystery at all. This is the reason for our tradition of unwritten precepts and practices, that the knowledge of our dogmas may not become neglected and contemned by the multitude through familiarity. "Dogma" and "Kerugma" are two distinct things; the former is observed in silence; the latter is proclaimed to all the world. One form of this silence is the obscurity employed in Scripture, which makes the meaning of "dogmas" difficult to be understood for the very advantage of the reader: Thus we all look to the East at our prayers, but few of us know that we are seeking our own old country, Paradise, which God planted in Eden in the East. Genesis 2:8. We pray standing, on the first day of the week, but we do not all know the reason. On the day of the resurrection (or "standing again" Grk. ἀνάστασις) we remind ourselves of the grace given to us by standing at prayer, not only because we rose with Christ, and are bound to "seek those things which are above," Colossians 3:1, but because the day seems to us to be in some sense an image of the age which we expect, wherefore, though it is the beginning of days, it is not called by Moses first, but one. For he says "There was evening, and there was morning, one day," as though the same day often recurred. Now "one" and "eighth" are the same, in itself distinctly indicating that really "one" and "eighth" of which the Psalmist makes mention in certain titles of the Psalms, the state which follows after this present time, the day which knows no waning or eventide, and no successor, that age which ends not or grows old. Of necessity, then, the church teaches her own foster children to offer their prayers on that day standing, to the end that through continual reminder of the endless life we may not neglect to make provision for our removal there. Moreover all Pentecost is a reminder of the resurrection expected in the age to come. For that one and first day, if seven times multiplied by seven, completes the seven weeks of the holy Pentecost; for, beginning at the first, Pentecost ends with the same, making fifty revolutions through the like intervening days. And so it is a likeness of eternity, beginning as it does and ending, as in a circling course, at the same point. On this day the rules of the church have educated us to prefer the upright attitude of prayer, for by their plain reminder they, as it were, make our mind to dwell no longer in the present but in the future. Moreover every time we fall upon our knees and rise from off them we show by the very deed that by our sin we fell down to earth, and by the loving kindness of our Creator were called back to heaven.

67. Time will fail me if I attempt to recount the unwritten mysteries of the Church. Of the rest I say nothing; but of the very confession of our faith in Father, Son, and Holy Ghost, what is the written source? If it be granted that, as we are baptized, so also under the obligation to believe, we make our confession in like terms as our baptism, in accordance with the tradition of our baptism and in conformity with the principles of true religion, let our opponents grant us too the right to be as consistent in our ascription of glory as in our

confession of faith. If they deprecate our doxology on the ground that it lacks written authority, let them give us the written evidence for the confession of our faith and the other matters which we have enumerated. While the unwritten traditions are so many, and their bearing on "the mystery of godliness," 1 Timothy 3:16, is so important, can they refuse to allow us a single word which has come down to us from the Fathers;—which we found, derived from untutored custom, abiding in unperverted churches;—a word for which the arguments are strong, and which contributes in no small degree to the completeness of the force of the mystery?

68. The force of both expressions has now been explained. I will proceed to state once more wherein they agree and wherein they differ from one another—not that they are opposed in mutual antagonism, but that each contributes its own meaning to true religion. The preposition "in" states the truth rather relatively to ourselves; while "with" proclaims the fellowship of the Spirit with God. Wherefore we use both words, by the one expressing the dignity of the Spirit; by the other announcing the grace that is with us. Thus we ascribe glory to God both "in" the Spirit, and "with" the Spirit; and herein it is not our word that we use, but we follow the teaching of the Lord as we might a fixed rule, and transfer His word to things connected and closely related, and of which the conjunction in the mysteries is necessary. We have deemed ourselves under a necessary obligation to combine in our confession of the faith Him who is numbered with Them at Baptism, and we have treated the confession of the faith as the origin and parent of the doxology. What, then, is to be done? They must now instruct us either not to baptize as we have received, or not to believe as we were baptized, or not to ascribe glory as we have believed. Let any man prove if he can that the relation of sequence in these acts is not necessary and unbroken; or let any man deny if he can that innovation here must mean ruin everywhere. Yet they never stop dinning in our ears that the ascription of glory "with" the Holy Spirit is unauthorized and unscriptural and the like. We have stated that so far as the sense goes it is the same to say "glory be to the Father and to the Son and to the Holy Ghost," and "glory be to the Father and to the Son with the Holy Ghost." It is impossible for any one to reject or cancel the syllable "and," which is derived from the very words of our Lord, and there is nothing to hinder the acceptance of its equivalent. What amount of difference and similarity there is between the two we have already shown. And our argument is confirmed by the fact that the Apostle uses either word indifferently—saying at one time "in the name of the Lord Jesus and by the Spirit of our God;" 1 Corinthians 6:11, at another "when you are gathered together, and my Spirit, with the power of our Lord Jesus," 1 Corinthians 5:4, with no idea that it makes any difference to the connection of the names whether he use the

conjunction or the preposition.

Chapter 28

That our opponents refuse to concede in the case of the Spirit the terms which Scripture uses in the case of men, as reigning together with Christ.

69. But let us see if we can bethink us of any defense of this usage of our fathers; for they who first originated the expression are more open to blame than we ourselves. Paul in his Letter to the Colossians says, "And you, being dead in your sins and the uncircumcision... has He quickened together with," Colossians 2:13. Christ. Did then God give to a whole people and to the Church the boon of the life with Christ, and yet the life with Christ does not belong to the Holy Spirit? But if this is impious even to think of, is it not rightly reverent so to make our confession, as They are by nature in close conjunction? Furthermore what boundless lack of sensibility does it not show in these men to confess that the Saints are with Christ, (if, as we know is the case, Paul, on becoming absent from the body, is present with the Lord, and, after departing, is with Christ) and, so far as lies in their power, to refuse to allow to the Spirit to be with Christ even to the same extent as men? And Paul calls himself a "labourer together with God," 1 Corinthians 3:9, in the dispensation of the Gospel; will they bring an indictment for impiety against us, if we apply the term "fellow-labourer" to the Holy Spirit, through whom in every creature under heaven the Gospel brings forth fruit? The life of them that have trusted in the Lord "is hidden," it would seem, "with Christ in God, and when Christ, who is our life, shall appear, then shall" they themselves also "appear with Him in glory;" Colossians 3:3-4, and is the Spirit of life Himself, "Who made us free from the law of sin," Romans 8:2, not with Christ, both in the secret and hidden life with Him, and in the manifestation of the glory which we expect to be manifested in the saints? We are "heirs of God and joint heirs with Christ," Romans 8:17, and is the Spirit without part or lot in the fellowship of God and of His Christ? "The Spirit itself bears witness with our spirit that we are the children of God;" and are we not to allow to the Spirit even that testimony of His fellowship with God which we have learned from the Lord? For the height of folly is reached if we through the faith in Christ which is in the Spirit hope that we shall be raised together with Him and sit together in heavenly places, whenever He shall change our vile body from the natural to the spiritual, and yet refuse to assign to the Spirit any share in the sitting together, or in the glory, or anything else which we have received from Him. Of all the boons of which, in accordance with the indefeasible grant of Him who has promised them,

we have believed ourselves worthy, are we to allow none to the Holy Spirit, as though they were all above His dignity? It is yours according to your merit to be "ever with the Lord," and you expect to be caught up "in the clouds to meet the Lord in the air and to be ever with the Lord." 1 Thessalonians 4:17. You declare the man who numbers and ranks the Spirit with the Father and the Son to be guilty of intolerable impiety. Can you really now deny that the Spirit is with Christ?

70. I am ashamed to add the rest. You expect to be glorified together with Christ; ("if so be that we suffer with him that we may be also glorified together;") Romans 8:17, but you do not glorify the "Spirit of holiness," Romans 1:4, together with Christ, as though He were not worthy to receive equal honor even with you. You hope to "reign with," 2 Timothy 2:12. Christ; but you "do despite unto the Spirit of grace," Hebrews 10:29, by assigning Him the rank of a slave and a subordinate. And I say this not to demonstrate that so much is due to the Spirit in the ascription of glory, but to prove the unfairness of those who will not ever give so much as this, and shrink from the fellowship of the Spirit with Son and Father as from impiety. Who could touch on these things without a sigh? Is it not so plain as to be within the perception even of a child that this present state of things preludes the threatened eclipse of the faith? The undeniable has become the uncertain. We profess belief in the Spirit, and then we quarrel with our own confessions. We are baptized, and begin to fight again. We call upon Him as the Prince of Life, and then despise Him as a slave like ourselves. We received Him with the Father and the Son, and we dishonour Him as a part of creation. Those who "know not what they ought to pray for," Romans 8:26 even though they be induced to utter a word of the Spirit with awe, as though coming near His dignity, yet prune down all that exceeds the exact proportion of their speech. They ought rather to bewail their weakness, in that we are powerless to express in words our gratitude for the benefits which we are actually receiving; for He "passes all understanding," Philippians 4:7, and convicts speech of its natural inability even to approach His dignity in the least degree; as it is written in the Book of Wisdom, "Exalt Him as much as you can, for even yet will He far exceed; and when you exalt Him put forth all your strength, and be not weary, for you can never go far enough." Verily terrible is the account to be given for words of this kind by you who have heard from God who cannot lie that for blasphemy against the Holy Ghost there is no forgiveness. Luke 12:10.

Chapter 29

Enumeration of the illustrious men in the Church who in their writings have used the word "with."

71. In answer to the objection that the doxology in the form "with the Spirit" has no written authority, we maintain that if there is no other instance of that which is unwritten, then this must not be received. But if the greater number of our mysteries are admitted into our constitution without written authority, then, in company with the many others, let us receive this one. For I hold it apostolic to abide also by the unwritten traditions. "I praise you," it is said, "that you remember me in all things, and keep the ordinances as I delivered them to you;" 1 Corinthians 11:2, and "Hold fast the traditions which you have been taught whether by word, or our Epistle." 2 Thessalonians 2:15. One of these traditions is the practice which is now before us, which they who ordained from the beginning, rooted firmly in the churches, delivering it to their successors, and its use through long custom advances pace by pace with time. If, as in a Court of Law, we were at a loss for documentary evidence, but were able to bring before you a large number of witnesses, would you not give your vote for our acquittal? I think so; for "at the mouth of two or three witnesses shall the matter be established." Deuteronomy 19:15. And if we could prove clearly to you that a long period of time was in our favor, should we not have seemed to you to urge with reason that this suit ought not to be brought into court against us? For ancient dogmas inspire a certain sense of awe, venerable as they are with a hoary antiquity. I will therefore give you a list of the supporters of the word (and the time too must be taken into account in relation to what passes unquestioned). For it did not originate with us. How could it? We, in comparison with the time during which this word has been in vogue, are, to use the words of Job, "but of yesterday." Job 8:9. I myself, if I must speak of what concerns me individually, cherish this phrase as a legacy left me by my fathers. It was delivered to me by one who spent a long life in the service of God, and by him I was both baptized, and admitted to the ministry of the church. While examining, so far as I could, if any of the blessed men of old used the words to which objection is now made, I found many worthy of credit both on account of their early date, and also a characteristic in which they are unlike the men of today—because of the exactness of their knowledge. Of these some coupled the word in the doxology by the preposition, others by the conjunction, but were in no case supposed to be acting divergently—at least so far as the right sense of true religion is concerned.

72. There is the famous Irenæus, and Clement of Rome; Dionysius

of Rome, and, strange to say, Dionysius of Alexandria, in his second Letter to his namesake, on "Conviction and Defence," so concludes. I will give you his very words. "Following all these, we, too, since we have received from the presbyters who were before us a form and rule, offering thanksgiving in the same terms with them, thus conclude our Letter to you. To God the Father and the Son our Lord Jesus Christ, with the Holy Ghost, glory and might for ever and ever; amen." And no one can say that this passage has been altered. He would not have so persistently stated that he had received a form and rule if he had said "in the Spirit." For of this phrase the use is abundant: it was the use of "with" which required defense. Dionysius moreover in the middle of his treatise thus writes in opposition to the Sabellians, "If by the hypostases being three they say that they are divided, there are three, though they like it not. Else let them destroy the divine Trinity altogether." And again: "most divine on this account after the Unity is the Trinity." Clement, in more primitive fashion, writes, "God lives, and the Lord Jesus Christ, and the Holy Ghost." And now let us hear how Irenæus, who lived near the times of the Apostles, mentions the Spirit in his work "Against the Heresies." "The Apostle rightly calls carnal them that are unbridled and carried away to their own desires, having no desire for the Holy Spirit," and in another passage Irenæus says, "The Apostle exclaimed that flesh and blood cannot inherit the kingdom of the heavens lest we, being without share in the divine Spirit, fall short of the kingdom of the heavens." If any one thinks Eusebius of Palestine worthy of credit on account of his wide experience, I point further to the very words he uses in discussing questions concerning the polygamy of the ancients. Stirring up himself to his work, he writes "invoking the holy God of the Prophets, the Author of light, through our Saviour Jesus Christ, with the Holy Spirit."

73. Origen, too, in many of his expositions of the Psalms, we find using the form of doxology "with the Holy Ghost." The opinions which he held concerning the Spirit were not always and everywhere sound; nevertheless in many passages even he himself reverently recognizes the force of established usage, and expresses himself concerning the Spirit in terms consistent with true religion. It is, if I am not mistaken, in the Sixth Book of his Commentary on the Gospel of St. John that he distinctly makes the Spirit an object of worship. His words are:—"The washing or water is a symbol of the cleaning of the soul which is washed clean of all filth that comes of wickedness; but none the less is it also by itself, to him who yields himself to the God-head of the adorable Trinity, through the power of the invocations, the origin and source of blessings." And again, in his Exposition of the Epistle to the Romans "the holy powers," he says "are able to receive the Only-begotten, and the Godhead of the Holy Spirit." Thus I apprehend, the powerful influence of tradition frequently impels men to express

themselves in terms contradictory to their own opinions. Moreover this form of the doxology was not unknown even to Africanus the historian. In the Fifth Book of his Epitome of the Times he says "we who know the weight of those terms, and are not ignorant of the grace of faith, render thanks to the Father, who bestowed on us His own creatures, Jesus Christ, the Saviour of the world and our Lord, to whom be glory and majesty with the Holy Ghost, forever." The rest of the passages may perhaps be viewed with suspicion; or may really have been altered, and the fact of their having been tampered with will be difficult to detect because the difference consists in a single syllable. Those however which I have quoted at length are out of the reach of any dishonest manipulation, and can easily be verified from the actual works.

I will now adduce another piece of evidence which might perhaps seem insignificant, but because of its antiquity must in nowise be omitted by a defendant who is indicted on a charge of innovation. It seemed fitting to our fathers not to receive the gift of the light at eventide in silence, but, on its appearing, immediately to give thanks. Who was the author of these words of thanksgiving at the lighting of the lamps, we are not able to say. The people, however, utter the ancient form, and no one has ever reckoned guilty of impiety those who say "We praise Father, Son, and God's Holy Spirit." And if any one knows the Hymn of Athenogenes, which, as he was hurrying on to his perfecting by fire, he left as a kind of farewell gift to his friends, he knows the mind of the martyrs as to the Spirit. On this head I shall say no more.

74. But where shall I rank the great Gregory, and the words uttered by him? Shall we not place among Apostles and Prophets a man who walked by the same Spirit as they; 2 Corinthians 12:18, who never through all his days diverged from the footprints of the saints; who maintained, as long as he lived, the exact principles of evangelical citizenship? I am sure that we shall do the truth a wrong if we refuse to number that soul with the people of God, shining as it did like a beacon in the Church of God; for by the fellow-working of the Spirit the power which he had over demons was tremendous, and so gifted was he with the grace of the word "for obedience to the faith among... the nations," Romans 1:5, that, although only seventeen Christians were handed over to him, he brought the whole people alike in town and country through knowledge to God. He too by Christ's mighty name commanded even rivers to change their course, and caused a lake, which afforded a ground of quarrel to some covetous brethren, to dry up. Moreover his predictions of things to come were such as in no wise to fall short of those of the great prophets. To recount all his wonderful works in detail would be too long a task. By the superabundance of gifts, wrought in him by the Spirit in all power and in signs and in marvels, he was

styled a second Moses by the very enemies of the Church. Thus in all that he through grace accomplished, alike by word and deed, a light seemed ever to be shining, token of the heavenly power from the unseen which followed him. To this day he is a great object of admiration to the people of his own neighbourhood, and his memory, established in the churches ever fresh and green, is not dulled by length of time. Thus not a practice, not a word, not a mystic rite has been added to the Church besides what he bequeathed to it. Hence truly on account of the antiquity of their institution many of their ceremonies appear to be defective. For his successors in the administration of the Churches could not endure to accept any subsequent discovery in addition to what had had his sanction. Now one of the institutions of Gregory is the very form of the doxology to which objection is now made, preserved by the Church on the authority of his tradition; a statement which may be verified without much trouble by any one who likes to make a short journey. That our Firmilian held this belief is testified by the writings which he has left. The contemporaries also of the illustrious Meletius say that he was of this opinion. But why quote ancient authorities? Now in the East are not the maintainers of true religion known chiefly by this one term, and separated from their adversaries as by a watchword? I have heard from a certain Mesopotamian, a man at once well skilled in the language and of unperverted opinions, that by the usage of his country it is impossible for any one, even though he may wish to do so, to express himself in any other way, and that they are compelled by the idiom of their mother tongue to offer the doxology by the syllable "and," or, I should more accurately say, by their equivalent expressions. We Cappadocians, too, so speak in the dialect of our country, the Spirit having so early as the division of tongues foreseen the utility of the phrase. And what of the whole West, almost from Illyricum to the boundaries of our world? Does it not support this word?

75. How then can I be an innovator and creator of new terms, when I adduce as originators and champions of the word whole nations, cities, custom going back beyond the memory of man, men who were pillars of the church and conspicuous for all knowledge and spiritual power? For this cause this banded array of foes is set in motion against me, and town and village and remotest regions are full of my calumniators. Sad and painful are these things to them that seek for peace, but great is the reward of patience for sufferings endured for the Faith's sake. So besides these let sword flash, let axe be whetted, let fire burn fiercer than that of Babylon, let every instrument of torture be set in motion against me. To me nothing is more fearful than failure to fear the threats which the Lord has directed against them that blaspheme the Spirit. Kindly readers will find a satisfactory defense in what I have said, that I accept a phrase so dear and so familiar to the

saints, and confirmed by usage so long, inasmuch as, from the day when the Gospel was first preached up to our own time, it is shown to have been admitted to all full rights within the churches, and, what is of greatest moment, to have been accepted as bearing a sense in accordance with holiness and true religion. But before the great tribunal what have I prepared to say in my defense? This; that I was in the first place led to the glory of the Spirit by the honor conferred by the Lord in associating Him with Himself and with His Father at baptism; Matthew 28:19, and secondly by the introduction of each of us to the knowledge of God by such an initiation; and above all by the fear of the threatened punishment shutting out the thought of all indignity and unworthy conception. But our opponents, what will they say? After showing neither reverence for the Lord's honor nor fear of His threats, what kind of defense will they have for their blasphemy? It is for them to make up their mind about their own action or even now to change it. For my own part I would pray most earnestly that the good God will make His peace rule in the hearts of all, so that these men who are swollen with pride and set in battle array against us may be calmed by the Spirit of meekness and of love; and that if they have become utterly savage, and are in an untamable state, He will grant to us at least to bear with long suffering all that we have to bear at their hands. In short "to them that have in themselves the sentence of death," 2 Corinthians 1:9, it is not suffering for the sake of the Faith which is painful; what is hard to bear is to fail to fight its battle. The athlete does not so much complain of being wounded in the struggle as of not being able even to secure admission into the stadium. Or perhaps this was the time for silence spoken of by Solomon the wise. Ecclesiastes 3:7. For, when life is buffeted by so fierce a storm that all the intelligence of those who are instructed in the word is filled with the deceit of false reasoning and confounded, like an eye filled with dust, when men are stunned by strange and awful noises, when all the world is shaken and everything tottering to its fall, what profits it to cry, as I am really crying, to the wind?

Chapter 30

Exposition of the present state of the Churches.

76. To what then shall I liken our present condition? It may be compared, I think, to some naval battle which has arisen out of time old quarrels, and is fought by men who cherish a deadly hate against one another, of long experience in naval warfare, and eager for the fight. Look, I beg you, at the picture thus raised before your eyes. See the rival fleets rushing in dread array to the attack. With a burst of uncontrollable fury they engage and fight it out. Fancy, if you like, the

ships driven to and fro by a raging tempest, while thick darkness falls from the clouds and blackens all the scenes so that watchwords are indistinguishable in the confusion, and all distinction between friend and foe is lost. To fill up the details of the imaginary picture, suppose the sea swollen with billows and whirled up from the deep, while a vehement torrent of rain pours down from the clouds and the terrible waves rise high. From every quarter of heaven the winds beat upon one point, where both the fleets are dashed one against the other. Of the combatants some are turning traitors; some are deserting in the very thick of the fight; some have at one and the same moment to urge on their boats, all beaten by the gale, and to advance against their assailants. Jealousy of authority and the lust of individual mastery splits the sailors into parties which deal mutual death to one another. Think, besides all this, of the confused and unmeaning roar sounding over all the sea, from howling winds, from crashing vessels, from boiling surf, from the yells of the combatants as they express their varying emotions in every kind of noise, so that not a word from admiral or pilot can be heard. The disorder and confusion is tremendous, for the extremity of misfortune, when life is despaired of, gives men license for every kind of wickedness. Suppose, too, that the men are all smitten with the incurable plague of mad love of glory, so that they do not cease from their struggle each to get the better of the other, while their ship is actually settling down into the deep.

77. Turn now I beg you from this figurative description to the unhappy reality. Did it not at one time appear that the Arian schism, after its separation into a sect opposed to the Church of God, stood itself alone in hostile array? But when the attitude of our foes against us was changed from one of long standing and bitter strife to one of open warfare, then, as is well known, the war was split up in more ways than I can tell into many subdivisions, so that all men were stirred to a state of inveterate hatred alike by common party spirit and individual suspicion. But what storm at sea was ever so fierce and wild as this tempest of the Churches? In it every landmark of the Fathers has been moved; every foundation, every bulwark of opinion has been shaken: everything buoyed up on the unsound is dashed about and shaken down. We attack one another. We are overthrown by one another. If our enemy is not the first to strike us, we are wounded by the comrade at our side. If a foeman is stricken and falls, his fellow soldier tramples him down. There is at least this bond of union between us that we hate our common foes, but no sooner have the enemy gone by than we find enemies in one another. And who could make a complete list of all the wrecks? Some have gone to the bottom on the attack of the enemy, some through the unsuspected treachery of their allies, some from the blundering of their own officers. We see, as it were, whole churches, crews and all, dashed and shattered upon the sunken reefs of

disingenuous heresy, while others of the enemies of the Spirit of Salvation have seized the helm and made shipwreck of the faith. 1 Timothy 1:19. And then the disturbances wrought by the princes of the world, 1 Corinthians 2:6, have caused the downfall of the people with a violence unmatched by that of hurricane or whirlwind. The luminaries of the world, which God set to give light to the souls of the people, have been driven from their homes, and a darkness verily gloomy and disheartening has settled on the Churches. The terror of universal ruin is already imminent, and yet their mutual rivalry is so unbounded as to blunt all sense of danger. Individual hatred is of more importance than the general and common warfare, for men by whom the immediate gratification of ambition is esteemed more highly than the rewards that await us in a time to come, prefer the glory of getting the better of their opponents to securing the common welfare of mankind. So all men alike, each as best he can, lift the hand of murder against one another. Harsh rises the cry of the combatants encountering one another in dispute; already all the Church is almost full of the inarticulate screams, the unintelligible noises, rising from the ceaseless agitations that divert the right rule of the doctrine of true religion, now in the direction of excess, now in that of defect. On the one hand are they who confound the Persons and are carried away into Judaism; on the other hand are they that, through the opposition of the natures, pass into heathenism. Between these opposite parties inspired Scripture is powerless to mediate; the traditions of the apostles cannot suggest terms of arbitration. Plain speaking is fatal to friendship, and disagreement in opinion all the ground that is wanted for a quarrel. No oaths of confederacy are so efficacious in keeping men true to sedition as their likeness in error. Every one is a theologue though he have his soul branded with more spots than can be counted. The result is that innovators find a plentiful supply of men ripe for faction, while self-appointed scions of the house of place-hunters reject the government of the Holy Spirit and divide the chief dignities of the Churches. The institutions of the Gospel have now everywhere been thrown into confusion by want of discipline; there is an indescribable pushing for the chief places while every self-advertiser tries to force himself into high office. The result of this lust for ordering is that our people are in a state of wild confusion for lack of being ordered; the exhortations of those in authority are rendered wholly purposeless and void, because there is not a man but, out of his ignorant impudence, thinks that it is just as much his duty to give orders to other people, as it is to obey any one else.

78. So, since no human voice is strong enough to be heard in such a disturbance, I reckon silence more profitable than speech, for if there is any truth in the words of the Preacher, "The words of wise men are heard in quiet," Ecclesiastes 9:17, in the present condition of things any

discussion of them must be anything but becoming. I am moreover restrained by the Prophet's saying, "Therefore the prudent shall keep silence in that time, for it is an evil time," Amos 5:13, a time when some trip up their neighbours' heels, some stamp on a man when he is down, and others clap their hands with joy, but there is not one to feel for the fallen and hold out a helping hand, although according to the ancient law he is not uncondemned, who passes by even his enemy's beast of burden fallen under his load. Ezekiel 23:5. This is not the state of things now. Why not? The love of many has waxed cold; Matthew 24:12, brotherly concord is destroyed, the very name of unity is ignored, brotherly admonitions are heard no more, nowhere is there Christian pity, nowhere falls the tear of sympathy. Now there is no one to receive "the weak in faith," Romans 14:1, but mutual hatred has blazed so high among fellow clansmen that they are more delighted at a neighbour's fall than at their own success. Just as in a plague, men of the most regular lives suffer from the same sickness as the rest, because they catch the disease by communication with the infected, so nowadays by the evil rivalry which possesses our souls we are carried away to an emulation in wickedness, and are all of us each as bad as the others. Hence merciless and sour sit the judges of the erring; unfeeling and hostile are the critics of the well disposed. And to such a depth is this evil rooted among us that we have become more brutish than the brutes; they do at least herd with their fellows, but our most savage warfare is with our own people.

79. For all these reasons I ought to have kept silence, but I was drawn in the other direction by love, which "seeks not her own," 1 Corinthians 13:5, and desires to overcome every difficulty put in her way by time and circumstance. I was taught too by the children at Babylon, that, when there is no one to support the cause of true religion, we ought alone and all unaided to do our duty. They from out of the midst of the flame lifted up their voices in hymns and praise to God, reeking not of the host that set the truth at naught, but sufficient, three only that they were, with one another. Wherefore we too are undismayed at the cloud of our enemies, and, resting our hope on the aid of the Spirit, have, with all boldness, proclaimed the truth. Had I not so done, it would truly have been terrible that the blasphemers of the Spirit should so easily be emboldened in their attack upon true religion, and that we, with so mighty an ally and supporter at our side, should shrink from the service of that doctrine, which by the tradition of the Fathers has been preserved by an unbroken sequence of memory to our own day. A further powerful incentive to my undertaking was the warm fervour of your "love unfeigned," and the seriousness and taciturnity of your disposition; a guarantee that you would not publish what I was about to say to all the world—not because it would not be worth making known, but to avoid casting pearls before swine. Matthew 7:6.

My task is now done. If you find what I have said satisfactory, let this make an end to our discussion of these matters. If you think any point requires further elucidation, pray do not hesitate to pursue the investigation with all diligence, and to add to your information by putting any uncontroversial question. Either through me or through others the Lord will grant full explanation on matters which have yet to be made clear, according to the knowledge supplied to the worthy by the Holy Spirit. Amen.

THE END

www.ingramcontent.com/pod-product-compliance
Lightning Source LLC
Chambersburg PA
CBHW031609040426
42452CB00006B/453